CHILDHOOD TODAY

Sara Miller McCune founded SAGE Publishing in 1965 to support the dissemination of usable knowledge and educate a global community. SAGE publishes more than 1000 journals and over 800 new books each year, spanning a wide range of subject areas. Our growing selection of library products includes archives, data, case studies and video. SAGE remains majority owned by our founder and after her lifetime will become owned by a charitable trust that secures the company's continued independence.

Los Angeles | London | New Delhi | Singapore | Washington DC | Melbourne

EDITED BY

ALEX OWEN

CHILDHOOD TODAY

Los Angeles | London | New Delhi
Singapore | Washington DC | Melbourne

Los Angeles | London | New Delhi
Singapore | Washington DC | Melbourne

SAGE Publications Ltd
1 Oliver's Yard
55 City Road
London EC1Y 1SP

SAGE Publications Inc.
2455 Teller Road
Thousand Oaks, California 91320

SAGE Publications India Pvt Ltd
B 1/I 1 Mohan Cooperative Industrial Area
Mathura Road
New Delhi 110 044

SAGE Publications Asia-Pacific Pte Ltd
3 Church Street
#10-04 Samsung Hub
Singapore 049483

Editor: Jude Bowen
Associate editor: George Knowles
Editorial assistant: Catriona McMullen
Production editor: Nicola Carrier
Copyeditor: Audrey Scriven
Proofreader: Jill Birch
Indexer: Silvia Benvenuto
Marketing manager: Lorna Patkai
Cover design: Wendy Scott
Typeset by: C&M Digitals (P) Ltd, Chennai, India
Printed in the UK

First published 2017

Library of Congress Control Number: 2017932943

British Library Cataloguing in Publication data

A catalogue record for this book is available from
the British Library

ISBN 978-1-47398-936-8
ISBN 978-1-47398-937-5 (pbk)

For Buddy, Grace and Bella

CONTENTS

ABOUT THE EDITOR AND CONTRIBUTORS

The editor

Alex Owen is Head of the Department and Senior Lecturer in Early Childhood at Liverpool Hope University. Her research focuses on the impact of poverty upon young children's current life experience and future life chances. She is a senior fellow of the HEA and vice-chair of governors at a local primary school.

The contributors

Babs Anderson is a lecturer in early childhood at Liverpool Hope University. Her research interests include young children's collaborative learning, the use of language as a cultural tool, and the co-construction of knowledge and understanding. She is the co-convenor of the Special Interest Group: Holistic Well-being of the European Early Childhood Education Research Association (EECERA).

Carol Aubrey is emeritus professor at the University of Warwick and Professorial Fellow at Liverpool Hope University. She trained and worked as a primary school teacher and educational psychologist before entering higher education. She has a long-term interest in children's policy and services, nationally and internationally, and has researched and published widely in this area.

Carolyn Blackburn is a senior research fellow in the Centre for Studies of Practice and Culture in Education at Birmingham City University. She is widely published in the field of inclusion and disability and has worked in early childhood education for nearly twenty years.

Marie Caslin is a lecturer in disability and education at Liverpool Hope University. Her research explores the position of young people identified as having 'behavioural problems' within the confines of the English education system. She is interested in gaining an understanding of the experiences of disabled children by listening to their voices.

Sue Cronin is acting head of the School of Teacher Education at Liverpool Hope University. Sue is an experienced teacher educator. She originally started in secondary mathematics before working for Liverpool LA as a school effectiveness officer. Since joining Hope she has worked across a variety of teacher education programmes.

Charlotte Jones is a senior lecturer in early childhood studies at Birmingham City University. Her recent research interests have focused on the policy-to-practice context to male professionals working in the field of early childhood education and care.

Rosemarie Lowe is head of department for childhood, youth and community at Birmingham City University. She has a long-term interest in the promotion of children's participation in the field of education, and in particular in how children can become active participants in researching their own educational lives.

Ged Mulhaney is currently developing and teaching an early years PGCE course at Liverpool Hope University. She is an experienced primary teacher with a range of senior management roles in early years, assessment and literacy. She has worked collaboratively with leadership teams and practitioners from PVIs, children's centres and schools.

Zoi Nikiforidou is a senior lecturer in early childhood at Liverpool Hope University. Her research interests relate to methodological and theoretical issues on teaching and learning, with an emphasis on the role of cognition, pedagogy and technology. She is also a member of OMEP UK and EECERA.

Theodora Papatheodorou is an international early childhood education consultant. She trained as a preschool teacher and worked in preschools, special education settings and in higher education, where she held various early childhood lecturing and research posts. She also worked for Save the Children UK, as Early Childhood Care and Development (ECCD) adviser, and for UNICEF as a freelance consultant.

Harriet Pattison is a lecturer in early childhood at Liverpool Hope University. She completed her PhD on how home-educated children learn to read and is interested in educational alternatives including differing constructions of childhood. Her current interests include informal learning and the philosophy of alternative education and literacy.

Michelle Pearson is acting head of initial teacher education at Liverpool Hope University. Previously she has taught as a primary school teacher with senior management responsibility and curriculum leadership expertise in literacy. She has also worked as a literacy consultant for two local authorities, working in partnership with schools to raise standards in literacy.

Erin Pritchard is a postdoctoral teaching fellow in disability and education at Liverpool Hope University. Her research interests include geographies of disability and geographies of body size, with a particular interest on how the built environment can be made accessible for people whose body size exceeds the norm.

Nina Sajaniemi is a principal investigator, adjunct professor (developmental neuropsychology) and head of early childhood education in the department of teacher education at the University of Helsinki. She is an experienced clinician in child neuropsychology and neuropsychotherapy. She has worked at the university hospital for the last twelve years.

Jim Stack is a lecturer in early childhood at Liverpool Hope University. His theoretical and research interests include how infants and preschoolers begin to understand that others may experience the world differently from themselves, and also how children use such understanding to engage in prosocial behaviours.

Laura Waite is a lecturer in disability studies at Liverpool Hope University following a career in education, health and social care. Some of her research is located at the intersection of disability studies and fat studies with a focus on how non-normative bodies are conceptualised and 'treated' as non-normative.

FOREWORD

This is an urgently needed book that explores a number of different concepts of childhood in the twenty-first century. It considers enduring topics and new concepts of childhood, and initiates a number of questions that students of education, childhood and early childhood studies can engage with as lines of inquiry. Structured around 10 chapters the book addresses contemporary and traditional constructions of childhood and approaches issues around the child, bringing to life theoretical perspectives and linking these to practice with interesting case studies. Important key debates such as the cotton wool generation, politics, poverty, equality and obesity are related to the impact of constructing our views of the child in today's society. The book offers a multidisciplinary approach of the child today that influences practice, policy and education, and offers diverse dimensions to provoke our thinking.

High-quality chapters help students to understand and question complex issues in childhood that are linked with the social problems experienced by children and faced by professionals. Critical and equally helpful, this book is an important contribution to an alternative view of the child which demonstrates how childhood is constructed today. It will be necessary reading for all students studying childhood and all professionals involved with children, as it offers different perspectives for both and discusses child-related situations that need special consideration.

Dr Ioanna Palaiologou, Institute of Education,
University College London

ACKNOWLEDGEMENTS

This book is the result of a Faculty of Education Research Seminar Series delivered at Liverpool Hope University. I would like to thank the Pro Vice-Chancellor (Academic) and Executive Dean of Education Revd Canon Professor Kenneth Newport for his support and encouragement regarding this project.

Thank you also to all of the chapter authors; the chapters are varied and clearly represent the multi-disciplinary nature of the study of childhood.

Many thanks to the brilliant team at SAGE, particularly to Jude Bowen and George Knowles.

Finally, thank you all of those researching, teaching and studying childhood studies – I hope that you find this book interesting and challenging!

PRAISE FOR THE BOOK

'This is an urgently needed book that explores a number of different concepts of childhood in the 21st century. The book throughout considers enduring topics and new concepts of childhood, and initiates a number of questions that students of education, childhood, and early childhood studies can engage as lines of inquiries. Structured around eleven chapters this book addresses contemporary and traditional constructions of childhood and approaches issues around the child, bringing to life theoretical perspectives and liking them to practice with interesting case studies. Important key debates such as the snowflake generation, politics, poverty, equality, and obesity are related to the impact of constructing our views of the child in today's society. The book offers a multidisciplinary approach of the child today that influences practice, policy, and education and offers diverse dimensions to provoke our thinking.'

'Throughout the book, the high quality chapters help students to understand and question complex issues in childhood that are linked with social problems experienced by children that children themselves and professionals are facing today. Critical and equally helpful, this book is an important contribution of alternative viewing of the child which demonstrates how childhood is constructed today. This book will be necessary reading for all studying childhood and all professionals involved with children as it offers different perspectives for studying children and childhood and discusses child related situations that need special consideration.'

Dr. Ioanna Palaiologou Institute of Education, University College London

'This book provides a detailed insight into different social constructs of childhood today. The subjects are definitely relevant for any student studying Early Childhood Studies and could also be used in other courses such as Education Studies. The reading is very approachable and very interesting, keeping the reader enthralled in the subject and at the same time deepening their knowledge and understanding. Incredibly useful for essays and exams!'

Amalie Quevedo, Early Childhood and Education Studies student, Liverpool Hope University

INTRODUCTION

ALEX OWEN

CHAPTER OBJECTIVES

- To communicate the aims and objectives of this book.
- To begin to consider the situation of the child today.
- To explore the use of labels and the impact they can potentially have on children's well-being.
- To elucidate the key components of the rest of the book and how they fit the overall direction of the argument presented.

The importance of the situation of children today is well recognised and is increasingly on the agenda of government departments and agencies worldwide. The construction of childhood is changing and the rate of this change is unprecedented. Advancement in technology has allowed children based in the United Kingdom to 'walk' through rainforests, communicate with astronauts in space and compete in real time in mathematics challenges with children in South Africa. Yet these developments have also allowed children to access inappropriate, indecent images and build 'friendships' with adults who have the worst intentions. Progression in mobility has allowed children to experience the beauty of diversity, explore cultures and traditions distinctly different from their own and learn about the importance of inclusion. Yet these developments have also exposed children to the prejudiced views of their neighbours and have forced them to live in a society just as divided as ever. Evolution of the structure of the family has supported a range of expressions of family, has mobilised the female workforce and has supported children to escape abusive family situations. Yet these developments have also resulted in significantly high rates of child poverty and more children than ever before experiencing parental separation. Changes in the reach of the media have raised awareness of the plight of children in war-torn countries, the trafficking of children across international borders and the potential of children to ensure a sustainable future. Yet these developments have also demonised children involved in acts of violence and labelled children who wear a 'hoodie' as trouble-making.

These changes in the social atmosphere that children inhabit have produced a construction of childhood for the 21st century that is profoundly different. The *United Nations Convention on the Rights of the Child* clearly articulates this new understanding (United Nations, 1989). This revolutionary, legally-binding, inter-national agreement affords all children civil, economic, social and cultural rights for the first time in history, revealing how the social construction of childhood has evolved. Children now have the right to life, survival and development; addi-tionally, they must be protected from violence, abuse and neglect. Children now have the right to an education and a future; furthermore, they must have the opportunity to be cared for by their parents or a guardian. Finally, and most con-troversially, children now have the right to express their thoughts and views; additionally, their opinions must be heard and taken into account. This interna-tional treaty sees the child as an individual worthy of value, and although implementation and enforcement are problematic, it seeks to ensure that within today's changing environment all children's basic needs are met to support each child to reach their full potential.

One of the key ways that this international mandate is implemented at a local level, within the United Kingdom, is through a focus on the well-being of the child. The constant change experienced by children in today's social atmosphere has been shown to have a significant impact upon their well-being (Earls and Carlson, 2001). 'Well-being' refers to the quality of a person's life (Hauser et al., 1997), and through a children's rights focus in terms of interventions, we expect children's well-being to be well supported in our 'advanced' society. Well-being can be meas-ured in terms of objective indicators, such as obesity rates or mental health measures. For instance, in the United Kingdom 19.1% of 10–11 year old children are termed as obese and 1 in 10 children aged 6–11 years have been diagnosed with a mental illness (Craig et al., 2015; Green et al., 2005). However, well-being can also be measured in terms of subjective indicators, involving children's life-satisfaction and their feelings of positive or negative emotion at various stages of childhood (The Children's Society, 2015). When measured in this way, it has been found that since 2008 children's life-satisfaction rates within the United Kingdom have stalled, with 5–10% of children resident in the United Kingdom expressing low levels of subjective well-being (The Children's Society, 2015). This is in contrast to an international perspective. When compared to 14 other countries across four continents (Algeria, Columbia, Estonia, Ethiopia, Germany, Israel, Nepal, Norway, Poland, Romania, South Africa, South Korea, Spain, and Turkey) England was placed 14th out of 15 for children's subjective views concerning their life satisfac-tion. Additionally, England was placed in the lower end of the rankings for 24 out of 30 aspects relating to childhood experience (Rees and Main, 2015). The links between subjective well-being and desirable outcomes for children are becoming well documented (Bradshaw et al., 2011; Bradshaw et al., 2013).

One way that the United Kingdom has sought to respond to this well-being focus, through policy creation and intervention development, is to break the child's life, being and experience down into component parts. The emphasis is often to inspect each part to make a diagnosis concerning 'what is wrong with them'. We use labels to define childhood. These labels, applied in the child's formative years, can have long-term implications on a child's present-day experience, as well as their future life chances. However, it is the argument of this book that these descriptions should firstly be understood but then challenged so that a child isn't limited by the parameters set. By studying the specifics of a certain aspect of today's construct of childhood and by understanding the label assigned, we can seek to explore the enhancement of the present-day life experience as well as the future life chances of the child in that respect. By understanding and exploring, yet challenging when appropriate, the pre-defined assumptions of the label assigned we can work towards the enhancement of the child's subjective experience of well-being.

CASE STUDY 1   EXPLORING A GOOD CHILDHOOD

The Children's Society has undertaken research into children's well-being in the United Kingdom. The *Good Childhood Report 2016* details some of these findings. The following includes excerpts from the report to provide an understanding of recent research into the well-being of children in the United Kingdom.

Key finding 1

A gender gap in some aspects of well-being has opened up in recent years, with girls becoming increasingly unhappy with their lives overall and with their appearance.

Girls are less happy than they used to be, with 1 in 7 (14%) 10–15 year old girls unhappy with their lives as a whole (up from 11% over a five-year period). By contrast, the proportion of boys of the same age who are unhappy with their lives as a whole has remained stable at 11%. This means the estimated number of girls in the UK who are unhappy with their lives has risen by 21% (from 234,300 to 283,200) between 2009/10 and 2013/14.

The difference is even starker when it comes to how children feel about the way they look. More than one third (34%) of girls are unhappy with their appearance (up from 30% over five years). By contrast, the proportion of boys of the same age who are unhappy with their appearance has remained stable at around 20%. This means the estimated number of girls in the UK who are unhappy with their appearance has risen by 8% (from 647,400 to 699,700) between 2009/10 and 2013/14.

This new trend builds on important findings from 2015's *Good Childhood Report* in which England ranked last out of 15 countries for happiness with appearance and also had the most pronounced gender differences of all participating countries (The Children's Society, 2016: 3).

(Continued)

(Continued)

Key finding 2

In this report, we combine measures of subjective well-being with a new measure of psychological well-being to assess the extent to which children are 'flourishing' in England today.

Although more than 8 out of 10 children (82%) are 'flourishing', 10% are 'languishing', having low scores for both subjective well-being and psychological well-being (The Children's Society, 2016: 3).

Key finding 3

As girls get older, they are more likely than boys to experience emotional problems such as anxiety and depression. Emotional problems are associated with happiness with appearance and life as a whole, and these links are stronger for girls than boys. Younger boys are more likely than girls to be unhappy with their school work and more likely to have conduct and hyperactivity/inattention problems. These problems are associated with happiness with school work, and these links are stronger for boys than girls.

These insights help to explain the finding that boys are more likely than girls to have a mental health problem at age 10 when all types are considered together – but by age 14 the situation is reversed (The Children's Society, 2016: 3).

The aim of this book is to provide a concise overview of some of the central aspects of children's contemporary experience, particularly within the United Kingdom, but with relation to international perspectives. In this respect, we shall explore some of the contemporary labels that we assign to the child, or use in discussion about children, in order to understand the reality and problematise assumptions that may be held.

In this respect we firstly, in Chapter 1, look at the idea of the **Cotton Wool Child**. The notion of the Cotton Wool Child has evolved from contemporary attitudes and policies reflecting the need to over-protect the vulnerable child. However, in this chapter we problematise this notion because risk can never be fully avoided and, to some extent, has been shown to be a necessary part of children's lives to support their holistic development. Nikiforidou argues in this chapter that experience of risk actually makes children 'risk experts' and she asserts the necessity to enhance this risk expertise by becoming risk literate. Instead of wrapping children in cotton wool to preserve and protect, the risk literate child can develop the ability to deal with uncertainty and assess risks in an appropriate fashion. By providing today's child with 'safely risky' opportunities to experiment, explore and learn, they are given the opportunity to thrive. Risk is understood to be complex and children need to remain safe. However, by developing risk literacy, rather than sheltering the child from all possible threat, it can foster their independence, awareness and capacity to deal with future situations.

In Chapter 2 we explore the **Selfish Child**. The conception of children is that they are self-focused and egocentric. However, in this chapter we explore a range of research studies that have provided insight into current understandings of sharing behaviours in young children. Previously, the child has been thought to exhibit non-sharing behaviours that are based upon egocentric self-regard, which is accompanied by an unconcerned lack of interest in the welfare of others. This view has informed our understanding of today's child as a Selfish Child. However, in this chapter Stack challenges this and asserts that the studies that have informed our view do not appropriately acknowledge the contextual conditions within which children most naturally engage with others. This leads to the labelling of children as selfish, as it suggests that preschool children, in particular, operate primarily from a basis of self-interest. This notion is critiqued and a different view of a prosocial, unselfish child, from the early preschool period, is presented.

In Chapter 3 we discuss the notion of the **Universal Child**. The *United Nations Convention on the Rights of the Child* (1989) has brought childhood to the forefront of national and international policies and has been instrumental in increasing government investment for services. This inevitably has led to the introduction of greater regulation, followed by child assessment, monitoring and evaluation, in order to establish quality of services and returns on investment. This leads to the concept of the Universal Child where all children are viewed in the same way. The chapter seeks to problematise this development and challenges the widespread use of universal child assessment to determine the quality of childhood services. Papatheodorou asserts that child assessment tools are largely developmental in nature, portraying a universal normative child, far removed from their context and cultural milieu. The notion that policies and assessment tools might influence and shape pedagogical praxis to form and mould today's universal child is challenged. Instead, this chapter presents the child as a unique and potent individual, far removed from a Universal Child, and asserts that, whilst educators are expected to frame their pedagogical praxis within existing policies and regulatory frameworks, there is also an ethical responsibility for making pedagogical choices that will ensure all children are treated as individuals.

In Chapter 4 the label of the **SEN/D Child** is critiqued. The position of disabled children has evolved throughout history and as a result of this the notion of a SEN/D Child has been constructed over time. Due to a continuous emphasis in contemporary society on 'normalising' childhood, anything outside of these very narrow realms is considered 'abnormal'. This leads to disabled children being 'othered' and thus disabled children are likely to encounter oppression throughout their childhood and beyond. It is the argument of this chapter that today's disabled children remain segregated from society; remaining excluded because they do not conform to 'normal' expectations. Caslin problematises this labelling of the SEN/D child as it leaves a significant number of children on the outskirts, not only in terms of their educational experiences, but also their wider social encounters. This chapter presents a challenge to remove this label that infers abnormality and to re-imagine our understanding of what it is to be 'normal'. By changing the culture of the education system and the attitudes of wider society the aspiration presented is to achieve authentic inclusion for all children.

In Chapter 5 we explore the **Regulated Child**. The *United Nations Convention on the Rights of the Child* (1989) has highlighted the importance of child voice and child participation. In this respect some children are supported to participate in decision making concerning their lives, although due to regulation this practice is uneven. In this chapter child participation is shown to be influenced by national policy and the agency involved, as well as the age and competence of the child concerned. Giving voice to children in their early years, as well as children with additional needs, disabled children and children with English as an additional language (EAL), poses particular challenges. In the chapter the impact of regulation on the child is explored, in particular in regard to child voice. Aubrey et al. highlight the fact that professional practice often prioritises the notion of the Regulated Child over child voice and participation. Yet it is shown that this prioritisation and resulting lack of involvement for the child can lead to a sense of increased powerlessness, contribute to lack of confidence and lower self-esteem.

In Chapter 6 we discuss the idea of the **Stressed Child**. The fundamental value of the education system should be to offer an experience of inclusion to all children. It should organise itself to accommodate the individually different developmental and biological needs of all children – one size never fits all. In this chapter, we explore the various needs of children generated by the fast-moving, ever-changing contemporary situation. Sajaniemi asserts that a child's response to contemporary society is not always the basis of a diagnosis nor the fault of the child. Instead she maintains that it is the shortcoming of adults to recognise the biological and emotional signals of the Stressed Child. Children signal their inner state continuously and search for answers to external stressors that provide positive feelings and manage negative ones. By creating a safe environment, which dampens overactive stress responses and helps the child to use their vagal brake, the notion of the perpetually Stressed Child is problematised. The chapter argues that pedagogically sensitive professionals can deliberately become sensitised to the needs of the children they work with.

In Chapter 7 we explore the notion of the **Political Child**. The desire for academic, and thus economic, success for future generations is at the foreground of UK education policy initiatives. Closely allied to this is the accompanying political drive to increase parental, in particular maternal, employment rates and the associated economic benefits in terms of potential increases in taxation and reduced welfare expenditure. The chapter sets out to consider some of the implications of this agenda for the Political Child through the lens of early years provision. Cronin et al. assert that the increased focus on more formally structured approaches to early years provision, with a linear hierarchy of skills designed to promote a pre-primary model, is contradictory to the neurological, social and developmental structures that would best be served by a later transition point to formal education. The sense of urgency at ensuring the development of high-quality childcare has continued to increase due to political drive and the focus on being 'ready' to succeed which underpin the political discourse of the current UK government. Garnering a social pedagogical approach to Early Years appears to elicit better results in long-term educational attainment, as seen in the Nordic countries of Finland and Norway, yet the politicisation of early years education and care in the United Kingdom represents a collective failure to focus on the here and now for this very important stage of childhood.

In Chapter 8 the idea of the **Natural Child** is examined. The notion of the child as natural has developed over time and is often perceived in contemporary under-standings with negative connotations. In this chapter we problematise the negative concept of the Natural Child as a socially constructed phenomenon which can be constructed and re-constructed in the light of new and changing ideas and con-cerns about nature as well as about children. For this reason, Pattison asserts that the Natural Child is a social construction in the same way that the child is a social construction. Due to this, there is no reason to think that changing ideas about childhood will make the concept of the natural child a redundant one. Instead, the natural child continues to have an important political salience and thus has value for the child in contemporary society.

In Chapter 9 the label of the **Poor Child** is discussed. Poverty has implications for a wide range of aspects relating to the child's life, including educational, health and socio-emotional outcomes. The inequality of experience for children living in poverty is revealed in their holistic development as early as 22 months of age. This disparity may then proliferate through each stage of childhood, resulting in a sig-nificant impact on a child's future life chances. This chapter problematises the concept of the Poor Child and seeks to challenge the outcomes for children living in deprived environments. Recent UK policy provides a range of objectives, in relation to the support of children living in poverty, but the application of these in relation to reducing the impact of poverty remains inconsistent across the diversity of local authority contexts. Anderson and Owen assert that providing external support for children and their families can lessen the negative impact of poverty upon chil-dren's present-day experience and their future life chances, ensuring that the Poor Child doesn't become the Poor Adult.

Finally, in Chapter 10, we explore the label of the **Fat Child**. The concept of childhood obesity is complex – much more so than the government, the media and the diet and fitness industries would have us believe. There are many forces at play and it is not as straightforward as merely asking all fat people to take up more physical activity or go on a diet. Additionally, we do not simply have fat children because they have 'bad parents'. In this chapter, we problematise the notion of the Fat Child and recognise that blaming individuals is much easier than tackling soci-etal issues, such as poverty and social inequality. Furthermore, we acknowledge the harm that is done to the well-being of children and their families through indi-vidual blame. Waite and Pritchard assert that in society fatness is perceived through the dominant discourse of obesity, where fatness is presented as blameworthy and easily rectified through diet and exercise. They provide a critique of this discourse as it relates to the Fat Child and seek to explore the negative effects it can have on fat children and their families.

CASE STUDY 2   EXPLORING KIRSTY'S EXPERIENCE

Kirsty went to live with her grandma when she was 7 years old. Her mum's new boyfriend had recently moved in with the family and this had unsettled Kirsty. Added to this, the focus on the three younger children in the home had left her feeling isolated and alone. These feelings of insecurity had manifested themselves in her behaviour at home, out in the local community and at school. She was a 'Problem Child'. Kirsty knew this label; she had heard family members and professionals talking about her 'problem' behaviour. She also believed this label, sometimes acting in such a way as to fulfil other people's negative expectations to gain the attention she so desperately craved.

Then Kirsty entered Miss Smith's class at school. Miss Smith refused to see the child as a problem. She refused to pigeon-hole Kirsty in the way that her label prescribed. She spent time with Kirsty. She didn't give up when Kirsty exhibited challenging behaviours; instead she tried to understand why. She took an interest in who Kirsty was – her talent for drawing, and mathematics, and cross country running. Slowly, there was a change. Once Kirsty had found an adult who refused to label her, and didn't have pre-defined ideas about who she was, she had the support she needed to explore who she wanted to be.

It is the assertion of this book that there is no such thing as a 'Problem Child'. A society that prescribes children pre-loaded labels without exploring the implications of those labels is the problem, as labels can direct the present and decide the future for the child involved. This book is written from the position that children are to be valued. The objective is to provoke listening and discussion with the aim of problematising the notion of labelling; to label is to negate the truly individual characteristics of the holistic child.

QUESTIONS FOR REFLECTION

1   The assertion of this chapter is that difference should be celebrated as a rich resource rather than a troublesome problem. The Poor Child, the Fat Child, the SEN/D Child, and the rest, all have great value. How can childhood settings authentically celebrate difference?

2   Parents are key partners in developing an authentic culture within a childhood setting where every child is valued and celebrated. How could practitioners develop this crucial relationship to ensure full participation?

3   Reflect on some of the labels you might assign to children, consciously or sub-consciously. How might these affect your engagement with them?

4   Reflecting on Case Study 2, consider the roles of the various adults in the situation. How could you summarise their attitudes concerning Kirsty? What impact did these attitudes have on her holistic well-being?

SUMMARY

How we understand childhood today is changing and the rate of this change is unprecedented. These changes have created a construction of childhood for the 21st century that is profoundly different. The United Nations Convention on the Rights of the Child seeks to inform our understanding of what it is to be a child today (United Nations, 1989); this is undertaken at a local level, within the United Kingdom, through a focus on child well-being. The social atmosphere, characterised by uncertainty, challenge and change, has been shown to have a significant impact upon children's well-being. In terms of their subjective well-being, in particular, children's life-satisfaction rates within the United Kingdom have been impeded. This is concerning as the links between subjective well-being and desirable outcomes for children are well documented. One way we have sought to respond to this well-being focus within the United Kingdom is to break the child down into component parts. We analyse each part of the child's life, being and experience to make a diagnosis concerning 'what is wrong with them' and then prescribe a label to define them. These labels, applied in the formative years, can have long-term implications for the child. Therefore, these descriptions should be understood so that they can be challenged, ensuring that a child isn't limited by the parameters set. By understanding and exploring, yet challenging when appropriate, pre-defined assumptions that are associated with a label, we can work towards the enrichment of the child's subjective experience of well-being.

Further reading

Beardsmore, R. and Siegler, V. (2014) *Measuring National Well-being – Exploring the Well-being of Children in the UK*. Newport: Office for National Statistics.

Bradshaw, J., Hoelscher, P. and Richardson, D. (2007) An index of child well-being in the European Union, 25, *Journal of Social Indicators Research*, 80: 133–177.

Rees, G. and Main, G. (eds) (2015) Children's Views on their Lives and Well-being in 15 countries: An Initial Report on the Children's Worlds Survey, 2013–14. York: Children's Worlds Project.

UNICEF Office of Research (2013) *Child Well-Being in Rich Countries: A Comparative Overview* (Innocenti Report Card 11). Florence: UNICEF Office of Research.

References

Bradshaw, J., Keung, A., Rees, G. and Goswami, H. (2011) Children's subjective well-being: international comparative perspectives, *Children and Youth Services Review*, 33 (4): 548–556.

Bradshaw, J., Martorano, B., Natali, L. and de Neubourg, C. (2013) Children's subjective well-being in rich countries, *Child Indicators Research*, 6 (4): 619–635.

Craig, R., Fuller, E. and Mindell, J. (eds) (2015) *Health Survey for England 2014*. London: The Health and Social Care Information Centre.

Earls, F. and Carlson, M. (2001) The social ecology of child health and well-being, *Annual Review of Public Health*, 22: 143–166.

Green, H., McGinnity, A., Meltzer, H., Ford T. and Goodman, R. (2005) *Mental Health of Children and Young People in Great Britain 2004*. London: Palgrave.

Hauser, R., Brown, B. and Prosser, W. (1997) *Indicators of Child Well-Being*. London: Sage.

Rees, G. and Main, G. (eds) (2015) Children's Views on their Lives and Well-being in 15 Countries: An Initial Report on the Children's Worlds Survey, 2013–14. York: Children's Worlds Project.

The Children's Society (2015) *The Good Childhood Report*. London: The Children's Society.

The Children's Society (2016) *The Good Childhood Report: Summary*. London: The Children's Society.

United Nations (1989) *United Nations Convention on the Rights of the Child* (UNCRC). Geneva: United Nations.

1

THE COTTON WOOL CHILD

ZOI NIKIFORIDOU

CHAPTER OBJECTIVES

- To explore issues related to safeguarding and 'over' protection.
- To underline how and why risk is a vital part of child development.
- To endorse the transition from the cotton wool child to the 'risk literate' child.
- To unpick the notion of risk literacy.

Risk and challenge are fundamental components of child development and well-being. Yet concerns for danger, injury, and the threat of modern societies have led to an increase in regulation and provision intending to ensure secure, risk-free environments. Nevertheless, the confrontation of risk does not only lie in adults' experience but is also a lifelong skill that may be fostered from early childhood through risk literacy. The aim of this chapter is to explore the position of risk in children's contemporary lives by drawing on the controversy between the cotton wool child and the 'risk expert' (Adams, 2006). It is proposed that besides safeguarding, there should be invested interest in supporting children to develop their own risk awareness and understanding of risk. Such implications signpost the importance of setting the foundations for risk literate children as present and future citizens in a sustainable, multimodal world.

Current trends and realities

In recent times, modern society has become a risk society in the sense that it is increasingly occupied with debating, preventing and managing the risks it has produced (Beck, 2006). New technology, socially-driven realities, increased urbanisation and mobility, environmental factors and various other 'stressors' characterise not only our own but also young children's lives. In response, adults try to guard and constrain any potential threats by providing young children with safe and stable environments. As such, in the majority world we frequently refer to the cotton wool child: the child who is wrapped up, by adults, as a fragile and precious parcel so as to be protected from any harm or danger. In this scenario, the adult undertakes the role of being the protector and guardian of young children, knowing and deciding for their needs, desires and best interests. In regard to child safeguarding or danger alerts or viewing children as vulnerable, immature, inexperienced and young (Munro, 2011), with 'specific' needs and rights to be met, adults carry out their responsibility as a duty of care and protection.

CASE STUDY 1.1   EXPLORING UK POLICY

The extracts below, from UK policy documents on safeguarding young children, illustrate the significance of safeguarding, the role of adults and the role of children in shaping a child-centred approach.

4. Safeguarding and promoting the welfare of children is defined for the purposes of this guidance as: protecting children from maltreatment; preventing impairment of children's health or development; ensuring that children grow up in circumstances consistent with the provision of safe and effective care; and taking action to enable all children to have the best outcomes.

(Source: DfE (2016) *Keeping Children Safe in Education: Statutory Guidance for Schools and Colleges.* London: DfE. p. 8.)

2. Safeguarding and promoting the welfare of children is everyone's responsibility. Everyone who comes into contact with children and their families and carers has a role to play in safeguarding children. In order to fulfil this responsibility effectively, all professionals should make sure their approach is child-centred. This means that they should consider, at all times, what is in the best interests of the child.

(Source: DfE (2016) *Keeping Children Safe in Education: Statutory Guidance for Schools and Colleges.* London: DfE. p. 8.)

22. Children want to be respected, their views to be heard, to have stable relationships with professionals built on trust and to have consistent support provided for their individual needs. This should guide the behaviour of professionals. Anyone working with children should see and speak to the child; listen to what they say; take their views seriously; and work with them collaboratively when deciding how to support their needs. A child-centred approach is supported by: the Children Act 1989 ... the Equality Act 2010 ... the United Nations Convention on the Rights of the Child (UNCRC).

(Source: DfE (2015) *Working Together to Safeguard Children: A Guide to Inter-agency Working to Safeguard and Promote the Welfare of Children.* London: DfE. p. 10.)

In response to policy, on many occasions adults tend to make decisions and inflict on children particular activities and lifestyles that are 'safe' and 'secure' through 'strict' regulations. They raise children under certain 'do's and don'ts' by attempting to control any possible source of harm, injury or risk. This overprotective attitude leads to one end of the spectrum, that of excessive regulations and policies where a 'no risk culture' is embedded. Bundy et al. (2009) highlight that this 'no risk' is a risk itself as it distorts and limits children's freedom to play by having negative implications for their well-being and growth. As a result, children have very little time to themselves and experience increasing adult surveillance. Wyver et al. (2010) agree that there is an overloaded 'surplus safety' today. Children are wrapped up in a blanket of caution, with limited occurrences for experimentation with the unknown. Their play and free time become supervised and monitored and their sense of adventure, freedom and inventiveness tends to be condensed; not just in the house, or the classroom, but in most places where children can be, for example, in playgrounds and in 'child friendly' public spaces.

In an attempt to explain this route of overprotection, Furedi (2005) refers to the crisis of adult identity. He questions the meaning of adulthood, especially in relation to children today. He argues that in some cases adults are viewed as a threat to children. There is a 'do not trust adults/strangers' attitude which in a way is misanthropic. There is this negative, mistaken predisposition in individualistic societies that adults cannot help but only abuse children. The sense of community or collectivism is vanishing and because of adult insecurities there seems to be a growing distance between adults and children. Adults tend to become estranged from children and have reached the point where, when children have problems, they are no longer sure if they should be involved in children's lives.

Nonetheless, even if matters are not at this extreme level, as Furedi (2005) implies, can systems and adult-driven decisions always eliminate risks? What about the cotton wool children themselves, their voices and their agency? Why, instead of overprotection, can't we trust children to work out their own risks? Why don't we support children in taking safe risks and initiatives?

Are children risk experts?

Adams (2006) mentioned that we are all true risk experts, in the sense that we have all been trained by practice in the management of risk. The development of our expertise in coping with uncertainty begins from infancy when we learn to crawl, walk, talk, ride a bicycle, handle sharp items and so on. Through trial and error processes, driven by curiosity and enjoyment, young children, like adults, perform a balancing act between the expected rewards of their actions against the perceived costs of their failures. Adams (2006) proposed the risk-thermostat model, asserting that everyone has a propensity to take risks. This propensity varies as perceptions of risk are influenced by experience. The more risks an individual takes the greater, on average, will be the losses and gains he or she incurs. Indeed, infants balance rewards and 'accidents' continuously through apprehension, determination and intense concentration.

Young children are relentless junior risk managers. Through their mistakes or achievements, they learn to cope with uncertainty and novelty, they experiment with familiar and unfamiliar surroundings, and in turn, they become creative, autonomous and decisive problem solvers (Ball, 2002; Tovey, 2007). They might fall down, lose or err, but then they will stand up and re-try, through remarkable persistence and resilience. By definition, growth involves taking risks and therefore risk-taking is a key element in children's well-being. It empowers their physical prowess and autonomy (Stephenson, 2003), their emotional awareness and regulation of sensation-seeking (Apter, 2007), their mastery over themselves and their surroundings (Nikiforidou et al., 2012), as well as their broader learning and development (Eichsteller and Holthoff, 2009) at a cognitive, social, emotional and biological level (Boyer, 2006).

Play provides opportunities for children to challenge themselves and their comfort zone. Through play they face possibilities, try out new ideas, emotions and actions, build independence and confidence, overcome conflicts with themselves and others and experience both failure and success. In particular, risky play is a key part of children's development from an evolutionary perspective as it has an adaptive function in reducing fear of stimuli and survival instincts and it is defined as 'thrilling and exciting forms of play that involve a risk of physical injury' (Sandseter and Kennair, 2011: 258). Play is not a risk-free activity (Thompson, 2005); it is a space for adventure, ingenuity, exploration, trophies, scars, bruises, disappointment and frustration. Sandseter (2007) has proposed six different categories of risky outdoor play that include high speeds, getting lost, dangerous elements, dangerous tools, great heights, and rough-and-tumble.

However, risk is not only physical. There are numerous situations and forms of risk that children, like everyone else, engage with. Specifically, children encounter emotional risks, social risks, personal risks and dilemmas in the course of their daily decisions. Through their relationships and interactions with others, through the development of their emotional regulation and self-awareness, through linguistic and communicative encounters, children confront risks and experiences led by uncertainty and experimentation. Under the 'initiative vs. guilt' stage proposed by Erikson (1950), during the ages of 3 to 6 years, children assert themselves more frequently and test their self-limits. At this stage, children are convinced that they *are* a person and they start finding out *what kind of* person they are going to be. According to Erikson (1950), children grow together both psychologically and physically; they begin to plan actions, make up games, approach what is desirable, initiate activities with others, and prepare for leadership and achievement roles:

> Both language and locomotion permit him to expand his imagination over so many things that he cannot avoid frightening himself with what he himself has dreamed and thought up. Nevertheless, out of all this he must emerge with a sense of unbroken initiative as a basis for a high, and yet realistic, sense of ambition and independence. (Erikson, 1968:115)

If this imagination, initiative or ambition is constantly hindered because of riskless, overly protective situations, then the child will not transit from what they may do to what they can do. They will not experience the consequences of their actions and choices. Instead, from a psychosocial perspective, they will develop a sense of guilt about their needs and desires and remain followers and risk-averters. Subsequently children, at this age, need to undergo self-activated experiences in order to become accustomed to discovery, mistakes and confidence.

How do children engage with risk?

Apart from their curiosity children, like adults and adolescents, might engage with risks for a number of reasons. Briefly, according to Morrongiello and Lasenby (2006), the factors that shape risk-taking can be individual characteristics (like temperament, personality, age, gender, cognition, emotions, motivations and prior experiences), family/parent influences (like parent modelling and beliefs, parenting style, sibling effects) and social-situational features (like peer interactions, media and immediate contextual demands). Likewise, Little (2006) agrees that age, gender, socialisation practices, personality traits and policy provisions are some of the components that characterise risk-taking tendencies in the early years. Therefore, attitudes and engagement with risk are both personally and socially constructed. As such, the cotton wool layer has elements based not only on adults' expectations, guidance and actions but also on children's personal knowledge and disposition towards risk. These spheres of influence are interconnected, or stitched together if we can picture a cotton wool blanket, and should be considered as equally important. Also, at different ages the weighting of these spheres of influence differs. For instance, during adolescence it is more likely for the personal construct of risk to dominate, leading to higher levels of risk-taking (Byrnes, 2003).

The differentiation between mentally confronting a risk and between either pursuing or avoiding a risk shows that there are two tiers or processes of risk (see Figure 1.1), one related to thinking and understanding risk (cognition) and the other related to acting upon risk (behaviour). Theoretically and empirically, risk

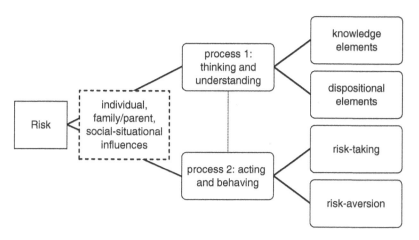

Figure 1.1 Risk and young children

perceptions and risky behaviours are strongly correlated in both negative and positive ways (Mills et al., 2008). Thus this correlation between thinking and doing is not always unidirectional. There are cases where, for instance, intuition (Fischbein, 1975) or heuristics and biases (Kahneman et al., 1982) or external factors like peer pressure come into play, leading to doing and then thinking or doing without thinking. Notwithstanding, the process of thinking and understanding, in relation to risk, can be fostered in young children (Nikiforidou et al., 2012).

From the cotton wool child to the risk literate child

Unquestionably, adults have a duty and responsibility to keep children safe and healthy as a matter of priority. A safe and welcoming environment is key to children's well-being and growth. As a consequence many provisions, regulations, policies and laws in the western world target, through a child-centred approach, child protection and safeguarding (i.e. DfE, 2016). The emerging dangers, stressors and alerts that dominate modern risk societies (Beck, 2006) can be considered as the main cause for cotton wool generations. Thus, to some extent, this upbringing has gone too far in over-emphasising what is risky (Thompson, 2005) and in cultivating a 'no risk' culture (Bundy et al., 2009). Under these circumstances children today grow up under 'surplus safety' experiences (Wyver et al., 2010); a reality that contradicts, in some cases, their human nature of 'surplus energy' and free exploration.

Whilst attempting to monitor and eliminate risk from children's lives, a considerate approach is to invest in their own knowledge and understanding of risk: in their becoming risk literate. If children are provided with a safe space to manage their own risks and decisions they will become more skilled, and subsequently literate, in confronting the unpredictable nature of the world, not only at that time but also later on in their lives (Gill, 2007). Risk literacy could be regarded as a way of supporting optimal child development while ensuring children's safety and well-being.

Education can play a significant role in transforming the cotton wool child into an agent who is able to cognitively manage risks (process 1) and act upon them (process 2). The main aims of risk education that apply to older children, according to Shearn (2004), which are those of raising children's risk awareness, of transferable skills and of behaviour modification, can be taken into account, at a certain level, from early in a child's education. Risk is complex by definition. However, it could be experiential, contextualised, meaningful and child-centred. Education, formal and informal, can play a vital role in supporting children in the process of becoming aware of risks and challenges. Consequently, the aim of risk education and, to be precise, of risk literacy is to enhance children's personal understanding of risk, its causes and its consequences. Recently, there has been emerging research interest in investigating how diverse pedagogical opportunities within children's daily routines can scaffold their learning about risk in its various forms and applications (Martignon and Krauss, 2009; Till, 2014; Lavrysen et al., 2015; Russell, 2015; Nikiforidou, 2017).

CASE STUDY 1.2   EXPLORING RECENT RESEARCH

One study explored a project named 'Riscki' that examined how children's risk perception and risk competence could be measured and developed. An intensive three-month training programme with risky-play activities was given to two classes of 4 and 6 year-old children in Belgium, while another two age-matched classes were used as control groups (N=87). Before and after the intervention period, quantitative and qualitative aspects of risk competence were assessed through: (1) a risk detection test (change detection paradigm); (2) teacher ratings; and (3) independent observers' qualitative ratings. The results indicated that a short-term intervention in the educational preschool context could enhance risk competence skills in very young children in the sense that it could develop their attention to and understanding of risk-related aspects. In addition, the outcome of this project has been linked to the development of pedagogical material that is available for schools, teachers and the community. Lastly, the researchers have called for larger-scale interventions and initiatives promoting a balanced and healthy development of risk competence from as early as preschool age.

(Source: Lavrysen et al. (2015) Risky-play at school: facilitating risk perception and competence in young children, *European Early Childhood Education Research Journal*, 10: 1–17.)

This study focuses on 8 to 10 year-old students (N=244) from Germany who participated in an intervention programme promoting risk literacy as a learning unit that consisted of four single maths lessons. In each lesson the students worked with hands-on material on proportional reasoning, the expected value, conditional probabilities and relative and absolute risks. There was a pre-test, a post-test and a follow-up test in each of the 12 classes that participated, both experimental and control. It was found that the intervention strengthened students' intuitions and fostered elementary competencies for risk assessment and probabilistic decision making. The researcher concluded with the position that risk and decision making under uncertainty could be a prevailing, exciting and meaningful topic with sustainable effects, as it could contribute to children's preparedness for the uncertainties of the modern technological world where the understanding of statistical information becomes more and more indispensable.

(Source: Till, C. (2014) Fostering risk literacy in elementary school, *Mathematics Education*, 9 (2): 83–96.)

A further study involved children (N=50) aged 5 to 6 years-old from Greece who were asked to identify and share their understanding of five risky activities based on Sandseter's (2007) categorisation of risky outdoor play. Semi-structured interviews and images as props were used in order to initiate these discussions and the children's responses showed their considerable capacity to reason in recognising causes (situational aspects of the contexts, the age of the actor and the natural hazards), consequences (physical harm) and causal

(Continued)

(Continued)

strength while comparing risky situations (considering the presence/absence of other/s). Such findings reveal that causal strength, probabilistic inference, future reasoning and linguistic capacity are strongly connected with children's reasoning and understanding of risk. In this direction, it is suggested that these aspects could inform the pedagogy of risk in the 'safe' early childhood classroom.

(Source: Nikiforidou, Z. (2017) 'It is riskier': preschoolers' reasoning of risky situations, *European Early Childhood Education Research Journal*, 25 (4).)

Risk literacy

Risk literacy implies the ability to deal with uncertainty in an informed way. It consists of lifelong skills that develop through the lifespan and entail perceptions (process 1) and responses (process 2) to risks. Risk literacy includes communicating, identifying and deciding whether to avoid or pursue a risk. Gigerenzer (2008) introduced this term and underlined that risk literacy is essential in our century where old certainties are rapidly altered or replaced by new ones. By providing children with opportunities to manage their own risks and decisions in the familiar environment of their classroom or setting, they gain experience in confronting unpredictability (Gill, 2007).

Risk literacy can resonate with two distinctive drivers. One has to do with the notion of multiliteracies in the 21st century. Being multi-literate aligns with being prepared to face change in a world characterised by local diversity and global connectiveness (O'Rourke, 2005). Risk-taking, criticality and creativity are crucial components in this world of multi-modality, technology and information. Having the capacity to judge and decide whether to take a risk or not, in diverse contexts of meaning, is a lifelong skill. As a matter of fact, risk literacy is as indispensable in the 21st century as reading and writing were, in terms of literacy, in the 20th century (Gigerenzer, 2008).

The other driver that underpins the necessity of risk literacy has to do with the UN sustainable development goal number 4, and in particular, target 4.7:

By 2030, ensure that all learners acquire the knowledge and skills needed to promote sustainable development, including, among others, through education for sustainable development and sustainable lifestyles, human rights, gender equality, promotion of a culture of peace and non-violence, global citizenship and appreciation of cultural diversity and of culture's contribution to sustainable development. (UN, 2015: 4.7)

Sustainable development implies stability and certainty that can be achieved if threats are confronted, and is defined as 'meeting the needs of the present without compromising the ability of future generations to meet their own needs' (WCED, 1987: 45). These needs can be met if reasonable decision making is implemented and avoidance or reduction of risks is taken into account. Children, as future generations, need to be equipped as early as possible with knowledge, skills and attitudes in dealing with change and uncertainty in regard to aspects of ecology, economy and equity; the three pillars of sustainable development.

Educational settings can contribute to cultivating a general can-do, risk-aware attitude. As Ungar (2007) proposes children should be provided opportunities to experience the four Cs: becoming *competent, caring contributors* to their *communities*. Competent in knowing their talents and capabilities, caring in showing their empathy, contributors in terms of self-efficacy and responsibility for a community that could be their friends, home, or any aspect of their outer world. Children should be empowered as thinkers, problem solvers and advocates of risk-taking when necessary. Learning about, making choices and acting on matters relevant to a just, healthy and sustainable life presupposes knowledge and competence in managing risks and change.

In practice-based terms, risk can be explored through a variety of 'curriculum subjects' and activities drawing upon personal, social, health and economic programmes (Rolfe, 2010). Risk can be connected to physical and health matters, to road traffic, to technology, to environmental issues, to aspects of social justice and so on. This cross-curricular, 'rounded' approach encourages meaningful learning (Hayes, 2010). Shearn (2004) claims that risk education can be embedded into existing schemes of work and reached through case studies, vignettes and practical activities. The integration of knowledge, ideas and concepts within and across subjects in relation to children's everyday experiences can support their risk awareness. For example, what are the risks of not placing our palm in front of our mouth when coughing (hygiene)? What are the risks for children who speak a different language (culture)? What are the risks of building a village close to the seaside (geography)? Usually risk literacy is linked to mathematics and statistics and therefore other parts of the curriculum are underpinned by risk-related concepts (Spiegelhalter, 2009; Eichler and Vogel, 2015). More research in this direction can shed light on how risk literacy can contribute in educational curricula and practices.

The basic argument is not to leave children totally exposed to any sort of hazard, but to allow them opportunities that would encourage self-care, risk appraisal and autonomous decision making (Christensen and Mikkelsen, 2008). Children need time and space to have their wishes and views heard on what is safe, dangerous, secure and risky. The solution of wrapping them up in cotton wool inhibits their capacity for innovation, imagination and opinion. Enhancing children's risk-awareness and risk-competence is a means of safeguarding them. Encouraging them to take reasonable and responsible risks when necessary, instead of overprotecting them, is a way forward.

QUESTIONS FOR REFLECTION

1. What is the relationship between safeguarding, risk and the cotton wool child?

2. How do you envisage the role of the adult (parent, practitioner, professional) in relation to the cotton wool child?

3. Do you agree that education can play a role in empowering children's risk awareness? Are there any obstacles or challenges in this respect?

4. Imagine you are a member of an educational consortium for early childhood. How would you argue in favour of risk literacy?

SUMMARY

The cotton wool child derives from attitudes and policies reflecting over-protection and excessive risk alarms. However, risks cannot be fully extinct and to some extent have to be part of children's lives and their holistic, psychosocial development and evolutionary growth. Experience makes children 'risk experts' and the proposal of this chapter underlines the necessity to enhance this expertise through the principles of risk literacy. Thus the risk-literate child can learn to face uncertainty and assess risks in a just and sustainable way, if given space and 'safely risk' opportunities to experiment, explore and learn. In the educational setting, through a cross-curricular approach, children can familiarise themselves with challenge and unfamiliarity, while building their personality through risky experiences, mistakes or achievements. Risk is complex and has many layers of influence; nonetheless, risk literacy is a stepping stone in fostering children's independence, awareness and capacity to deal with the unknown in judging whether to engage with a risk or avoid it.

End of chapter glossary

- **Risk** involves situations where there is possibility of harm or damage instead of the intended gain or opportunity.
- **Risk literacy** refers to an individual's knowledge, understanding and engagement with risk.
- **Risk society** describes a society occupied with debating, preventing and managing risk.
- **Safeguarding** covers the measures put in place to protect children from maltreatment and ensure their well-being.

Further reading

Lee, E., Bristow, J., Faircloth, C. and Macvarish, J. (2014) *Parenting Culture Studies*. Basingstoke: Palgrave Macmillan.
Gigerenzer, G. (2014) *Risk Savvy: How To Make Good Decisions*. New York: Viking.

References

Adams, J. (2006) *Risk*. London: Routledge.

Apter, M.J. (2007) *Danger: Our Quest For Excitement*. Oxford: Oneworld.

Ball, D. (2002) *Playgrounds: Risks, Benefits and Choices*. Middlesex University: HSE Books.

Beck, U. (2006) Living in the world risk society, *Economy and Society*, 35 (3): 329–345.

Boyer, T. (2006) The development of risk-taking: a multi-perspective review, *Developmental Review*, 26 (3): 291–345.

Bundy, A.C., Luckett, T., Tranter, P.J., Naughton, G.A., Wyver, S., Spies, G. and Ragen, J. (2009) The risk is that there is 'No Risk': a simple innovative intervention to increase children's activity levels, *International Journal of Food Science and Technology*, 17: 33–45.

Byrnes, J. (2003) 'Changing Views on the Nature and Prevention of Adolescent Risk Taking'. In D. Romer (ed.), *Reducing Adolescent Risk: Toward an Integrated Approach*. Thousand Oaks, CA: Sage.

Christensen, P. and Mikkelsen, M.R. (2008) Jumping off and being careful: children's strategies of risk management in everyday life, *Sociology of Health & Illness*, 30 (1): 112–130.

DfE (2015) *Working Together to Safeguard Children: A Guide to Inter-agency Working to Safeguard and Promote the Welfare of Children*. London: DfE.

DfE (2016) *Keeping Children Safe in Education: Statutory Guidance for Schools and Colleges*. London: DfE.

Eichler, A. and Vogel, M. (2015) Teaching risk in school, *The Mathematics Enthusiast*, 12 (1): 168–183.

Eichsteller, G. and Holthoff, S. (2009) Risk competence: towards a pedagogic conceptualization of risk, *Children Webmag*, 9.

Erikson, E.H. (1968) *Identity, Youth, and Crisis*. New York: Norton.

Erikson, J.M. (1950) 'Growth and Crises of the Healthy Personality'. In E.H. Erikson and J.E. Senn Milton (eds), *Symposium on the Healthy Personality*. Oxford: Josiah Macy Jr. Foundation.

Fischbein, E. (1975) *The Intuitive Sources of Probabilistic Thinking in Children*. Dordrecht: Reidel.

Furedi, F. (2005) 'Making Sense of Child Safety: Cultivating Suspicion'. In S. Waiton and S. Baird (eds), *Cotton Wool Kids? Making Sense of 'Child Safety'*. Glasgow: Generation Youth Issues.

Gigerenzer, G. (2008) *Rationality for Mortals: How People Cope With Uncertainty*. Oxford: Oxford University Press.

Gill, T. (2007) *No Fear: Growing Up in a Risk Averse Society*. London: Calouste Gulbenkian Foundation.

Hayes, D. (2010) The seductive charms of a cross-curricular approach, *Education 3-13: International Journal of Primary, Elementary and Early Years Education*, 38 (4): 381–387.

Kahneman, D., Slovic, P. and Tversky, A. (eds) (1982) *Judgment Under Uncertainty: Heuristics and Biases*. New York: Cambridge University Press.

Lavrysen, A., Bertrands, E., Leyssen, L., Smets, L., Vanderspikken, A. and De Graef, P. (2015) Risky-play at school: facilitating risk perception and competence in young children, *European Early Childhood Education Research Journal*, 10: 1–17. DOI: 10.1080/1350293X.2015.1102412.

Little, H. (2006) Children's risk-taking behaviour: implications for early childhood policy and practice, *International Journal of Early Years Education*, 14: 141–154.

Martignon, L. and Krauss, S. (2009) Hands-on activities for fourth graders: a tool box for decision-making and reckoning with risk, *International Electronic Journal of Mathematics Education*, 4 (3): 227–258.

Mills, B., Reyna, V.F. and Estrada, S. (2008) Explaining contradictory relations between risk perception and risk taking, *Psychological Science*, 19 (5): 429–433.

Morrongiello, B. and Lasenby, J. (2006) Finding the daredevils: development of a sensation seeking scale for children that is relevant to physical risk taking, *Accident Analysis and Prevention*, 38: 1101–1106.

Munro, E. (2011) *The Munro Review of Child Protection: Final Report. A child-centred system*. London: Department for Education.

Nikiforidou, Z. (2017) 'It is riskier': preschoolers' reasoning of risky situations, *European Early Childhood Education Research Journal*, 25 (4).

Nikiforidou, Z., Pange, J. and Chadjipadelis, T. (2012) Risk literacy in early childhood education under a lifelong perspective, *Procedia – Social and Behavioral Sciences*, 46: 4830–4833.

O'Rourke, M. (2005) 'Multiliteracies for 21st Century Schools'. In ANSN (ed.), *Snapshot*. Lindfield, NSW: The Australian National Schools Network Ltd.

Rolfe, H. (2010) *Learning to Take Risks, Learning to Succeed*. London: National Endowment for Science, Technology and the Arts.

Russell, G.L. (2015) Risk education: a worldview analysis of what is present and could be, *The Mathematics Enthusiast*, 12 (1): 62–84.

Sandseter, E. (2007) Categorizing risky play: how can we identify risk-taking in children's play?, *European Early Childhood Education Research Journal*, 15 (2): 237–252.

Sandseter, E. and Kennair, L. (2011) Children's risky play from an evolutionary perspective: the anti-phobic effects of thrilling experiences, *Evolutionary Psychology*, 9: 257–284.

Shearn, P. (2004) *Teaching Practice in Risk Education for 5-16 Year Olds*. Health and Safety Laboratory: Report Number HSL 2005/23.

Spiegelhalter, D. (2009) Probability lessons may teach children how to weigh life's odds and be winners, *The Times*, 5 January.

Stephenson, A. (2003) Physical risk-taking: dangerous or endangered?, *Early Years*, 23 (1): 35–43.

Thompson, S. (2005) 'Risky Play'. In S. Waiton and S. Baird (eds), *Cotton Wool Kids: Making Sense of Child Safety*. Glasgow: Generation Youth Issues.

Till, C. (2014) Fostering risk literacy in elementary school, *Mathematics Education*, 9 (2): 83–96.

Tovey, H. (2007) *Playing Outdoors: Spaces and Places, Risk and Challenge*. Maidenhead: Open University Press.

Ungar, M. (2007) *Too Safe For Their Own Good*. Toronto: McClelland and Stewart.

United Nations (2015) *Sustainable Development Goals*. [online] https://sustainable development.un.org/sdg4 (last accessed 20 October 2016).

World Commission on Environment and Development (WCED) (1987) *Our Common Future*. Oxford: Oxford University Press.

Wyver, S., Tranter, P., Naughton, G., Little, H., Sandseter, E.B.H. and Bundy, A. (2010) Ten ways to restrict children's freedom to play: the problem of surplus safety, *Contemporary Issues in Early Childhood*, 11 (3): 263–277.

2

THE SELFISH CHILD

JIM STACK

CHAPTER OBJECTIVES

- To describe research that assesses sharing behaviours in young children.

- To present research findings related to merit-based sharing in young children.

- To explore theory of mind during the preschool period.

- To gain an understanding of the relationship between theory of mind and sharing behaviours during early childhood.

Do nothing from selfishness or empty conceit, but with humility of mind regard one another as more important than yourselves; do not merely look out for your own personal interests, but also for the interests of others. (*Philippians* 2: 3–4)

This verse, taken from the New Testament of the Bible, is a useful starting point when considering the topic of selfishness in young children. We only need to pause for a moment to consider that there are strong social, moral, ethical and religious pressures to act in non-selfish ways. Adults, for the most part at least, conform to social standards and thus usually engage with others in non-selfish ways (Fehr and Fischbacher, 2003). There is a popular notion that children are selfish in nature, however our understanding of selfish and other-regarding behaviour during infancy, early and middle childhood appears far from straightforward. There is evidence which suggests that infants within the second year of life have an understanding of what is fair and unfair (Geraci and Surian, 2011; Sloane et al., 2012; Sommerville et al., 2013). There is also evidence from studies using child-friendly versions of the dictator game and the ultimatum game (to be presented in detail in Case Study 2.1) which demonstrate that forms of understanding become manifested in a range of fairness and sharing behaviours by the age of around 6 or 7 years (e.g. Fehr et al., 2008).

The broad developmental landscape provided here raises an interesting question about how children, particularly those aged between 3 and 6 years-old, allocate resources to others and whether they are selfish in this respect. Researchers (e.g. Olson and Spelke, 2008; Moore, 2009) demonstrate that under certain circumstances, such as when sharing with friends or close acquaintances, children are capable of offering equitable divisions of resources to other parties. However, many studies assessing preschoolers' sharing behaviours support the view that young children are for the most part selfish (e.g. Thompson et al., 1997; Blake and Rand, 2010; Gummerum et al., 2010).

CASE STUDY 2.1   EXPLORING THE DICTATOR GAME AND THE ULTIMATUM GAME

Research assessing young children's understanding of fairness and sharing has emerged from game theory methodologies used in behavioural economics research with adults (e.g. Güth et al., 1982; Henrich et al., 2005; Engel, 2011). Of the many methods developed in this field two have been used quite extensively within developmental research with young children, namely the dictator game and the ultimatum game.

A typical example of the dictator game (DG) is as follows: one adult (the proposer) is given a predetermined amount of resources (e.g. £10) and told that they can keep the full amount for themself or share some or all of it with a second person (the receiver) who they will never meet. The key point about this game is that the receiver must accept the offer given, even if this is a very low offer (e.g. the proposer keeps £9 for himself and only offers £1 to the receiver).

If we work from an economic model, based purely on self-interest, then it follows that proposers in the dictator game should offer £0 to the receiver and keep the maximum amount of £10 for themselves. Findings from a meta-analysis by Engel (2011) demonstrate that 36% of proposers in these studies did not share any of their resources. This, however, demonstrates that approaching two thirds of adult proposers shared some of their windfall with the receiver. Furthermore, the average offer made by proposers in this analysis was 28% of the resources available to them (Camerer, 2003).

The ultimatum game (UG) (Güth et al., 1982) follows the same rationale as the dictator game but adds a further level of complexity. In UG studies the proposer is provided with the same scenario as above, but informed that if the receiver is not happy with the amount they are offered then the receiver can reject this 'unfair' offer and both parties (the proposer and receiver) will give all the money back to the experimenter, resulting in no one getting anything! As expected, proposers typically offer more resources than they do in dictator game trials with the average offer being between 30 and 40% of the available resources and rejection rates typically high for offers less than 20% (Camerer and Thaler, 2005). This higher rate of offers can be related to a fear of reprisals from an unhappy receiver.

When viewed together the findings from these two games suggest that the mechanisms underpinning sharing behaviours in human adults are complex.

On the one hand, there is evidence from the UG that adults are motivated by self-interest and a fear of punishment and therefore employ strategy-based approaches to maximise personal gain. On the other hand, there is also evidence in adults that they consistently demonstrate 'other-regarding preferences' and act in non-selfish ways even when there is no personal or reputational cost to themselves (List, 2007).

The impact of collaboration and merit

Earlier it was argued that studies testing preschoolers' rates of sharing (e.g. Thompson et al., 1997; Blake and Rand, 2010; Gummerum et al., 2010) support the view that children are, for the most part, selfish. Importantly, these studies have emerged from and utilised child-friendly versions of the methodologies used with adults. In contrast to these 'windfall' approaches, Tomasello and colleagues (e.g. Hamann et al., 2011, 2014; Warneken et al., 2011; Melis et al., 2013; Tomasello and Vaish, 2013) argue that a more appropriate measure of how younger children share should be consistent with the evolutionary mechanisms that were responsible for the emergence of early collaborative hunter-gatherer societies. In outlining this position and in providing a critique Tomasello and Vaish state:

these experimental studies involved windfall situations in which a child is given some resources by a third party without having to work for them and must relinquish some resources to demonstrate fairness. Such situations are removed from the evolutionary mechanisms that we believe likely shape these phenomena in early ontogeny. Our hypothesis is that from early in ontogeny, children's sharing and fairness-related behaviours should reflect the effects of the collaborative foraging context of early humans, in which one shares the spoils equally among those who took part in the collaborative effort. We thus argue that prior work has underestimated children's sensitivity to equality because it has not provided the relevant context. (2013: 243)

Evidence consistent with this statement is provided by Hamann et al. (2011). This comparative study assessed the impact of collaborative, parallel-work or no-work (windfall generation of resources) activities on subsequent sharing behaviour with 2 and 3 year-olds. The findings show that collaboration, when contrasted with parallel-work or no-work (windfall) conditions, facilitated more equal rates of sharing in 3 year-olds, and in some instances children as young as 2 years. In a similar study Melis et al. (2013) assessed 3 year-olds' rates of sharing with a partner who had either actively collaborated or expressed a wish not to be involved in a rope-pulling task that resulted in the acquisition of resources. The findings from this study again demonstrated that task collaboration facilitated a more equal division of these resources when compared with the lower rates of sharing evidenced in the 'free-riding' condition.

As well as collaboration, another factor that appears to facilitate greater levels of sharing during early development is the principle of merit. The traditional view is that our understanding of the relationship between merit and sharing does not emerge until the school years or beyond (Hook and Cook, 1979; Gummerum et al., 2008). Kanngiesser and Warneken provide an overview of these issues and an account of the early developmental model devised to conceptualise our early understanding of this relationship:

> Children are thought to go through three major developmental stages: young children are purely selfish, older children follow a strict equality rule (everyone gets the same, irrespective of individual contributions), and school-aged children begin to take individual contributions into account ('merit' or 'equity'). (2012: 1)

In contrast to the above statement there is evidence from infancy research using a violation of expectation (VOE) looking time approach which demonstrates early sensitivity to the relationship between sharing and merit. VOE looking time designs are based on the argument that infants will look longer at surprising or unexpected behaviour than unsurprising or expected events (Haith, 1998; Aslin, 2007). Research found that 20 month-olds looked longer at events where one character had worked harder than the other yet both characters were rewarded equally. Moving into the period of early preschool Baumard et al. (2012) demonstrated that 3 year-olds expected that a character, who had worked to the completion of a task (baking cookies), deserved more than a second character who had lost interest in the task and stopped. While these findings are important, they only assess children's understanding of merit-based sharing from a third-party perspective where the children themselves are not affected by the outcome.

Taking a different approach to this question Hamann, Bender and Tomasello (2014) provided a first-person assessment of the relationship between relative merit and resource allocation in collaborative and non-collaborative contexts with a sample of 3.5 year-olds. In this study children were paired and worked either collaboratively or in a parallel-work task (non-collaboration) which involved pulling ropes in order to obtain rewards. During these tasks, in both the collaborative and parallel work conditions, one of the children was also given extra work to do in order to succeed on the task, whereas the other child had no extra work to do. Children were then allocated resources in an unequal manner. In the 'deserving condition' (high merit) the child who had performed the extra work was given three toys (this larger allocation matched the extra work performed) and the second child only received one toy. In the 'underserving condition' (low merit) this distribution of toys was reversed (which meant that the child who had performed the extra work only received one toy whereas the child who had not performed the extra work obtained three toys). The key findings from this study showed that children in the underserving condition shared more than in the deserving condition only when this had been situated within a collaborative context. These findings highlight that meritocratic sharing, which involves sharing according to the work performed, is evident at this earlier developmental period when framed within collaborative contexts.

A first-person approach was also taken by Kanngiesser and Warneken (2012) with a sample of 3 to 5 year-olds. The key findings from this study showed that children's allocation of rewards to themselves varied depending on the amount of work they had contributed relative to their partner. Although children rarely offered more than half of their reward they were willing to take a smaller amount in trials where they had contributed less than their co-worker.

These findings provide an important step in bettering our understanding of the contextual factors related to sharing behaviours in preschoolers. However, there may be other factors which influence how children decide what is fair or unfair when dividing resources with a co-worker. For example, the relationship between relative merit and equitable sharing is based on the premise that people who work hard (provide greater effort and productivity) deserve a bigger slice of the reward than people who work less hard (Bediou et al., 2012). However, despite the fact that the co-worker may deserve an equal slice of a jointly earned reward there is no guarantee that such equitable behaviour will be forthcoming. On the one hand, the person who is dividing the joint earnings may have no clear understanding of how a selfish act (keeping more for themselves) may impact on their co-worker. Alternatively, this person may be fully aware of how the other person would feel and think but acts selfishly regardless. This suggests that an understanding of how other people think and feel may influence more equitable rates of sharing in situations where a co-worker has (high merit) or has not (low merit) contributed to the acquisition of jointly earned resources.

CASE STUDY 2.2   EXPLORING JACK'S EXPERIENCE – CONTEXTUALISING MERIT-BASED SHARING

Scenario 1: One autumn two friends, Jack and Ray, advertise in a local shop that they are available at evenings and weekends to help out in the local community with small odd jobs, such as clearing leaves from gardens or washing neighbours' cars. They get a response from a neighbour who has asked them to tidy up leaves in the garden. They are told that the job should last no longer than a couple of hours and that they will be given a reward of £1 for every bag of leaves they clear. Their neighbour shows them how to use the requisite tools and then leaves them to perform the task. The children set to work, however, after only a short period of time it becomes apparent that one of the children is not working to the same level as the other child. After an hour Jack has finished his half of the garden, but Ray has barely managed to make any progress and says that he wants to go home as he is cold (see Baumard et al. (2012) for an empirical assessment of this situation). Ray then leaves and Jack is left to finish off the task on his own. At the end of the task he has filled 10 bags. The neighbour says he is very happy with the work and gives Jack £10.

Scenario 2: Jack then decides that he does not want to work with Ray anymore and so approaches Eric, his other friend, to see if he would be interested in doing odd jobs with him. He agrees and the next day they get a call from a different

(Continued)

(Continued)

neighbour and spend their Saturday afternoon working together clearing his garden. They both work hard and contribute equally to the task. Upon completion Eric says he has to rush home as his dinner is ready and that Jack should pick up their earnings from their neighbour. The neighbour gives Jack £10.

These two scenarios provide Jack with a dilemma: how much of the £10 should he share in each instance? The commonly held view is that Jack should assess the relative merit of both co-workers and therefore share the money in an equitable manner (Bediou et al., 2012). Therefore, it would seem reasonable for Jack to offer Eric half of the money (50%) but offer Ray a much smaller percentage (perhaps 20% if he is feeling generous). This division of resources is, however, by no means set in stone. For example, if we focus on Jack's work with Eric, Jack may take a self-interested approach and only offer him a smaller percentage of the money, perhaps 20%, and keep 80% for himself. Such behaviour would be deemed by most as being selfish. However, there may be more than one reason for behaving in such a way. On the one hand, Jack may make an informed, calculated decision and perform this selfish action with full awareness, but little regard, for how his friend will feel. Alternatively, Jack's selfish decision may be influenced by his inability to fully appreciate how Eric would feel. These outcomes are related to Jack's understanding of how Eric may think or feel – Jack's theory of mind.

Theory of mind

One way that can be used to assess this question is the child's emerging social understanding, or what is widely known as having a 'theory of mind' (ToM). This is defined as the ability to attribute mental states to self and others (Wellman et al., 2001) and encompasses an understanding of intentions, desires, emotions, beliefs and other internal states. There is some controversy about how these various forms of social understanding emerge across infancy (Allen, 2015). However, there is clear evidence that infants from the first year of life have an understanding of others' goals and intentions (Woodward, 1998; Behne et al., 2005). For example, Behne et al. (2005) demonstrate that from around 9 months of age infants will respond less favourably to an adult who is unwilling, rather than unable, to pass them a toy. This suggests that infants have an understanding of the intentions which underlie actions. In terms of desire-state understanding, Repacholi and Gopnik (1997) demonstrate that 18 month-olds are able to reason as, upon request, infants at this age provided an adult with the adult's desired food, rather than provide them with the food the child themself liked.

Apart from these 'lower level' forms of social understanding, evidence suggests that an understanding of false belief, which is considered by many as the litmus test of social understanding, does not emerge until around 4 years of age (Wellman et al., 2001). However, under certain circumstances children younger than this have also demonstrated such understanding (Garnham and Ruffman, 2001).

Children's understanding of false belief has been measured by tests such as the Unexpected Transfer/Sally-Anne Task (Wimmer and Perner, 1983; Baron-Cohen et al., 1985) and the Unexpected Contents Task (Hogrefe et al., 1986). In the Unexpected Transfer Task Sally takes a toy and puts it inside Location A. She then leaves. While she is gone Anne takes the toy and places it inside Location B. Sally arrives back and the child is asked where Sally will look for her toy. For many people reading this the correct answer may appear quite straightforward – Sally will look for it in Location A. However, there is much more involved in providing an accurate response to this question. In order to arrive at this answer the respondent must suspend their own egocentric view of reality, which involves the fact that they have seen it move from Location A to Location B, and also put themself into someone else's shoes and 'mentally represent' how the other person would experience the situation.

Making connections between theory of mind and sharing behaviours

In case study 2.2 it was argued that the decision to share equally with another child may be underscored by a child's theory of mind. Importantly, this relationship between theory of mind and sharing behaviours has recently been demonstrated in preschool research (Takagishi et al., 2010; Wu and Su, 2014). Takagishi et al. (2010) assessed this relationship using the Unexpected Transfer/Sally-Anne task and a child-friendly version of the Ultimatum Game with 5 year-old Chinese children. The findings from this study demonstrated that children who passed the false belief task offered significantly more resources to a second child than those children who did not pass this test. While these findings are both interesting and important there are limitations within this study. Firstly, some studies have demonstrated that under Ultimatum Game conditions the receiver can feel emotions such as disgust if a low offer is provided from the proposer (Chapman et al., 2009). Therefore, these rates of sharing may also result from a more strategy-based approach, designed to reduce feelings of embarrassment or guilt, rather than due to a more benign, prosocial motive (List, 2007).

Wu and Su (2014) provide a further assessment of the relationship between social understanding and sharing in a sample of 72 Chinese 2 to 4 year-olds. In order to assess theory of mind this study employed a Chinese version of the Wellman scale (Wellman and Liu, 2004; Wellman et al., 2006) to assess diverse desires and beliefs, knowledge access, false belief and real-apparent emotion. The sharing task in Wu and Su's (2014) study involved children experiencing requests that began with a comment phase for a small selection of various objects. Here the experimenter stated 'these are so cool'. This statement was repeated twice and if no items were shared the experiment then entered the desire phase. Here the experimenter stated 'I like these toys! I have none. I want to play with them'. If no items were forthcoming, the experiment then entered a request phase. Here the experimenter stated 'Would you please give me some to play with?' There were a number of interesting findings from this study. Firstly, younger children (2 and 3 year-olds) relied more on communicative cues provided by the experimenter in order to demonstrate sharing behaviours. In contrast the 4 year-olds shared more spontaneously with the experimenter. More importantly, and regardless of the age of the child, these findings demonstrate that children, who have a greater sense of theory of mind, as seen by higher score on the diverse beliefs and knowledge access tasks, engage in higher rates of sharing.

These findings shed some further light on the relationship between theory of mind and sharing. However, there may be some further limitations to this study. Firstly, it might be argued that through providing a request for items children in this study may have felt compelled to share, even if they privately wish to keep resources for themselves. Secondly, and applicable also to the findings from Takagishi et al. (2010), this study assessed children's sharing behaviours in a culture that emphasises collectivism and low individualism (Hofstede, 1984). Therefore, it may be argued that rates of sharing would alter if these studies were replicated with children from individualised western societies. In support of this argument Rochat and colleagues (e.g. Rochat et al., 2009; Robbins et al., 2016) demonstrate that children from the US are more inclined to 'self-hoard' resources when compared with children from less individualised societies (e.g. Peru, China and Tibet).

A further concern with previous findings regarding the assessment of theory of mind and sharing (Takagishi et al., 2010; Wu and Su, 2014) is based on querying the 'windfall' approach. Therefore, we still know very little about three key areas related to this approach; firstly, how preschoolers in the United Kingdom use either the collaboration or work ethic (the relative merit) of another person as a basis for sharing; secondly, whether such children utilise their emerging understanding of other's mental states (theory of mind) in such interactions; and finally, whether sharing rates and use of theory of mind varies across cultures.

In a first step toward understanding these issues Schäfer, Haun and Tomasello (2015) assessed the relationship between work production and sharing behaviours across three cultures. Two of the groups of children tested were from remote rural and sparsely populated egalitarian and partial hunter-gatherer societies in Namibia. The third sample of children were from a typical German town with a population of around 24,000 people. In this study children worked in pairs in order to 'fish out' magnetic cubes from two small containers to acquire a corresponding number of rewards. In the unequal merit condition, which was rigged, one child fished out 75% of the cubes, whereas the other child only fished out 25%. In two control conditions children, firstly, fished out an equal amount of cubes (equal merit) or, secondly, were given an unequal division of cubes. These researchers hypothesised that German children may employ a sharing strategy founded on work-based merit and therefore are perhaps more inclined to keep more resources in this condition, whereas the children from the African samples may focus less on work-based merit and instead apply the principle of equality in their sharing behaviours. The findings from this study support these assertions in that the German children shared proportionally based on the relative contributions of each child in the work-based merit condition. In contrast, African children, mirroring cultural practices within their societies, placed much less emphasis on the role of merit and distributed resources in a far more equal manner.

In outlining their interpretation of these findings Schäfer et al. state:

> Cultural differences might stem from a variety of factors. We propose that our data could at least in part be explained by the fact that in large-scale societies (e.g. Germany), relationship-neutral norms might be particularly important for regulating transactions between individuals who do not share personal history or interact only temporarily in specific contexts. In such cultures, a focus on equitable interactions, especially when distributing resources that are produced through joint efforts, gains importance, as there may be no future encounters in which things could be evened out. In contrast, in many small-scale societies most exchanges take place between individuals familiar with one another and who repeatedly interact in various domains ... In such societies, norms applied to interactions might be more dependent on personal relationships than on impersonal standards. Thus, in such cultures, it may be more important to build and sustain long-term relationships based on equity than to establish equity within any single interaction. (2015: 1258–1259)

In summarising these points it can be seen that our current understanding of sharing during the preschool period is still fairly limited. We do now know that children share far more equally where prior collaboration is evident or under conditions of relative merit. We also know that such rates of sharing behaviours are culturally specific. Finally, we have recent emerging evidence demonstrating that preschoolers use their understanding of others' mental states (theory of mind) when engaging in sharing behaviours. In terms of future directions, we now require further research that assesses the relationship between theory of mind and sharing under conditions of collaboration and merit across different cultures.

QUESTIONS FOR REFLECTION

1. Consider examples from your own experience with young children. What instances can you recall where children have been selfish or generous with their resources? What activities could children engage in in order to facilitate sharing behaviours?

2. In what ways do young children use their understanding of others' mental states (theory of mind) – intentions, desires and false beliefs – in their interactions with other people? In what ways do they use their emerging theory of mind as a basis for prosocial acts, such as being fair, demonstrating empathy and helping others?

3. Consider ways in which children's theory of mind may be advanced through social interaction. What factors may influence the emergence of such forms of understanding?

SUMMARY

The studies looked at in this chapter provide a fascinating insight into our current understanding of sharing behaviours in young children. In the opening section of this chapter a biblical quote was cited, which began with the statement 'Do nothing from selfishness or empty conceit'; this quote then states, 'do not merely look out for your own personal interests, but also for the interests of others' (*Philippians* 2: 3–4). If taken literally this statement suggests that non-sharing behaviours are based upon egotistical self-regard, which is accompanied by an unconcerned lack of interest in the welfare of others. If viewed alongside studies that do not appropriately acknowledge the contextual conditions within which children most naturally engage with others, this would suggest that preschool children operate primarily from a basis of self-interest – i.e. they are selfish. A further factor which may also impede our view of a prosocial, unselfish child is that the early preschool period sees the emergence of the types of understanding (theory of mind) required to demonstrate other-regarding preferences during this period and beyond.

End of chapter glossary

- **False belief** involves an understanding held by an individual about a situation that is in contrast with reality.
- **Merit-based sharing** takes place when merit is taken into account when sharing out resources.
- **Selfish** can be defined as a human trait that lacks consideration for others.
- **Sharing** involves dividing an item and giving a portion of this item to someone else.
- **Theory of mind** is the ability to attribute mental states to oneself and to others through an understanding of intention, desires, emotions and beliefs.

Further reading

Hamann, K., Bender, J. and Tomasello, M. (2014) Meritocratic sharing is based on collaboration in 3-year-olds, *Developmental Psychology*, 50: 121–128.

Takagishi, H., Kameshima, S., Schug, J., Koizumi, M. and Yamagishi, T. (2010) Theory of mind enhances preference for fairness, *Journal of Experimental Child Psychology*, 105: 130–137.

Tomasello, M. and Vaish, A. (2013) Origins of human cooperation and morality, *Annual Reviews of Psychology*, 64: 231–255.

References

Allen, J. (2015) How to help: Can more active behavior measures help transcend the infant false-belief debate? *New Ideas in Psychology*, 39: 63-72.

Aslin, R.N. (2007) What's in a look?, *Developmental Science*, 10 (1): 48–53.

Baron-Cohen, S., Leslie, A.M. and Frith, U. (1985) Does the autistic child have a 'theory of mind?', *Cognition*, 21: 37–46.

Baumard, N., Mascaro, O. and Chevallier, C. (2012) Preschoolers are able to take merit into account when distributing goods, *Developmental Psychology*, 48: 492–498.

Bediou, B., Sacharin, V., Hill, C., Sander, D. and Scherer, K.R. (2012) Sharing the fruit of labor: flexible application of justice principles in an ultimatum game with joint-production, *Social Justice Research*, 25(1): 25–40.

Behne, T., Carpenter, M., Call, J. and Tomasello, M. (2005) Unwilling versus unable: infants' understanding of intentional action, *Developmental Psychology*, 41: 328–337.

Blake, P.R. and Rand, D.G. (2010) Currency value moderates equity preference among young children, *Evolution and Human Behavior*, 31: 210–218.

Camerer, C. (2003) *Behavioral Game Theory: Experiments in Strategic Interaction*. New York: Sage.

Camerer, C. and Thaler, R.H. (1995) Anomalies: ultimatums, dictators and manners, *Journal of Economic Perspectives*, 9(2): 209–219.

Chapman, H.A., Kim, D.A., Susskind, J.M. and Anderson, A.K. (2009) In bad taste: evidence for the oral origins of moral disgust, *Science*, 323: 1222–1226.

Engel, C. (2011) Dictator games: a meta study, *Experimental Economics*, 14: 583–610.

Fehr, E., Bernhard, H. and Rockenbach, B. (2008) Egalitarianism in young children, *Nature*, 454: 1079–1083.

Fehr, E. and Fischbacher, U. (2003) The nature of human altruism, *Nature*, 425: 785–791.

Garnham, W.A. and Ruffman, T. (2001) Doesn't see, doesn't know: is anticipatory looking really related to understanding of belief?, *Developmental Science*, 4 (1): 94–100.

Geraci, A. and Surian, L. (2011) The developmental roots of fairness: infants' reactions to equal and unequal distributions of resources, *Developmental Science*, 14: 1012–1020.

Gummerum, M., Hanoch, Y. and Keller, M. (2008) When child development meets economic game theory: an interdisciplinary approach investigating social development, *Human Development*, 51 (4): 235–261.

Gummerum, M., Hanoch, Y., Keller, M., Parsons, K. and Hummel, A. (2010) Preschoolers' allocations in the dictator game: the role of moral emotions, *Journal of Economic Psychology*, 31: 25–34.

Güth, W., Schmittberger, R. and Schwarze, B. (1982) An experimental analysis of ultimatum bargaining, *Journal of Economic Behavior and Organization*, 3: 367–388.

Haith, M.M. (1998) Who put the cog in infant cognition? Is rich interpretation too costly?, *Infant Behavior and Development*, 21: 167–179.

Hamann, K., Bender, J. and Tomasello, M. (2014) Meritocratic sharing is based on collaboration in 3-year-olds, *Developmental Psychology*, 50: 121–128.

Hamann, K., Warneken, F., Greenberg, J.R. and Tomasello, M. (2011) Collaboration encourages equal sharing in children but not in chimpanzees, *Nature*, 476 (7360): 328–331.

Henrich, J., Boyd, R., Bowles, S., Camerer, C.F., Fehr, E., Gintis, H., McElreath, R., Alvard, M., Barr, A., Ensminger, J., Henrich, N., Hill, K., Gil-White, F., Gurven, M., Marlowe, F.W., Patton, J.Q. and Tracer, D. (2005) Economic man in cross-cultural perspective: behavioral experiments in 15 small-scale societies, *Behavioral and Brain Sciences*, 28: 795–855.

Hofstede, G. (1984) *Culture's Consequences: International Differences in Work-related Values*. Beverly Hills, CA: Sage.

Hogrefe, J., Wimmer, H. and Perner, J. (1986) Ignorance versus false belief: a developmental lag in attribution of epistemic states, *Child Development*, 57: 567–582.

Hook, J.G. and Cook, T.D. (1979) Equity theory and the cognitive ability of children, *Psychological Bulletin*, 86 (3): 429–445.

Kanngiesser, P. and Warneken, F. (2012) Young children consider merit when sharing resources with others, *PLoS One*, 7 (8): e43979.

Lewis, C. and Osborne, A. (1990) Three-year-olds' problems with false belief: conceptual deficit or linguistic artefact?, *Child Development*, 61: 1514–1519.

List, J.A. (2007) On the interpretation of giving in dictator games, *Journal of Political Economy*, 115 (3): 482–492.

Melis, A., Altricher, K., Schneider, A. and Tomasello, M. (2013) Allocation of resources to collaborators and free-riders by 3-year-olds, *Journal of Experimental Child Psychology*, 114: 364–370.

Moore, C. (2009) Fairness in children's resource allocation depends on the recipient, *Psychological Science*, 20: 944–948.

Olson, K.R. and Spelke, E.S. (2008) Foundations of cooperation in young children, *Cognition*, 108: 222–231.

Repacholi, B.M. and Gopnik, A. (1997) Early reasoning about desires: evidence from 14- and 18-month-olds, *Developmental Psychology* 33 (1): 12–21.

Robbins, E., Starr, S. and Rochat, P. (2016) Fairness and distributive justice by 3-5 year-old Tibetan children, *Journal of Cross-Cultural Psychology*, 47 (3): 333–340.

Rochat, P., Dias, M.D.G., Liping, G., Broesch, T., Passos-Ferreira, C., Winning, A. and Berg, B. (2009) Fairness in distributive justice by 3- and 5-year-olds across seven cultures, *Journal of Cross-Cultural Psychology*, 40: 416–442.

Schäfer, M., Haun, D. and Tomasello, M. (2015) Fair is not fair everywhere, *Psychological Science*, 26: 1252–1260.

Sloane, S., Baillargeon, R. and Premack, D. (2012) Do infants have a sense of fairness?, *Psychological Science*, 23: 196–204.

Sommerville, J.A., Schmidt, M.F.H., Yun, J. and Burns, M. (2013) The development of fairness expectations and prosocial behavior in the second year of life, *Infancy*, 18: 40–66.

Takagishi, H., Kameshima, S., Schug, J., Koizumi, M. and Yamagishi, T. (2010) Theory of mind enhances preference for fairness, *Journal of Experimental Child Psychology*, 105: 130–137.

Thompson, C., Barresi, J. and Moore, C. (1997) The development of future-oriented prudence and altruism in preschoolers, *Cognitive Development*, 12: 199–212.

Tomasello, M. and Vaish, A. (2013) Origins of human cooperation and morality, *Annual Reviews of Psychology*, 64: 231–255.

Warneken, F., Lohse, K., Melis, A.P. and Tomasello, M. (2011) Young children share the spoils after collaboration, *Psychological Science*, 22: 267–273.

Wellman, H.M., Cross, D. and Watson, J. (2001) Meta-analysis of theory-of-mind development: the truth about false belief, *Child Development*, 72: 655–684.

Wellman, H.M., Fang, F., Liu, D., Zhu, L. and Liu, G. (2006) Scaling of theory-of-mind understandings in Chinese children, *Psychological Science*, 17: 1075–1081.

Wellman, H.M. and Liu, D. (2004) Scaling of theory-of-mind tasks, *Child Development*, 75: 523–541.

Wimmer, H. and Perner, J. (1983) Beliefs about beliefs: representation and constraining function of wrong beliefs in young children's understanding of deception, *Cognition*, 13: 103–128.

Woodward, A.L. (1998) Infants selectively encode the goal object of an actor's reach, *Cognition*, 69: 1–34.

Wu, Z. and Su, Y. (2014) How do preschoolers' sharing behaviors relate to their theory of mind understanding?, *Journal of Experimental Child Psychology*, 120: 73–86.

3

THE UNIVERSAL CHILD

THEODORA PAPATHEODOROU

CHAPTER OBJECTIVES

- To discuss research evidence that has informed international and national childhood policies.

- To explore how such policies and regulatory frameworks portray the image of the universal normative child, an image that is far removed from the geopolitical, socio-economic and cultural influences upon a child in a given place at a given time.

- To propose a pedagogical approach that ensures each and every child reaches their full potential, cultivates their capabilities and asserts their individuality through just and fair educational entitlement.

The image of the universal child, as portrayed in developmental theories, has long been contested by academics, researchers and practitioners alike. Yet this image remains dominant in international and national childhood policies and regulatory frameworks that inevitably influence expectations about children's learning and development, as well as the pedagogical practices for achieving them.

The chapter draws upon research evidence from different fields of study (e.g. neuroscience, evaluation of early childhood programmes and economics) and the principles of the *United Nations Convention on the Rights of the Child* (UNCRC, 1989), and is framed within the debate of equity in education, arguing for a pedagogical approach that seeks to support the unique and individual child.

Care and provision

Traditionally, provision for children was divided into care and education, with the first viewed mainly as the responsibility of and funded by parents, and the latter being considered as a public good funded by the State. Where publicly funded care was offered, this was mainly for families in receipt of welfare support. By the turn of the 21st century, however, the policy landscape for early childhood provision in particular had changed by integrating education and care. This was reflected in international declarations and commitments. For example, in the 1990s the Jomtien declaration 'Education for All' affirmed that education starts at birth (UNESCO, 1990), and a decade later UNESCO adopted the expansion and improvement of early childhood care and education as its primary goal (UNESCO, 2000). The interactional nature of care and education was explicitly embraced in the 'Moscow Framework for Action and Collaboration', which called for multi-sectorial collaboration for achieving children's holistic development (UNESCO, 2010). Currently, early childhood care and education is at the forefront of the global development agenda, with the Sustainable Development Goals (SDGs) having a specific education target requiring countries to 'by 2030, ensure that all girls and boys have access to quality early childhood development, care and pre-primary education so that they are ready for primary education' (UN, 2015: SDG 4.2).

Research evidence, particularly from neuroscience and brain development, as well as the evaluation and economic analysis of early childhood programmes, together with the *United Nations Convention on the Rights of the Child* (UNCRC, 1989), provided the impetus needed for early childhood care and education to be at the forefront of international and national policies and the global development agenda. An overview of the research is included below, followed by a discussion of its influence on early childhood policy in particular.

The child as the productive citizen of tomorrow

As we shall see in detail in Chapter 6, neuroscience and brain development research has shown that early adverse experiences, such as family stress, neglect, exposure to violence, corporal punishment and limited stimulation (especially during the first three years of life) impact negatively on brain architecture. This in turn affects sensory, cognitive and behaviour functions that determine children's learning and future academic success (NSCDC, 2010). For instance, children who are subject to under-nutrition, especially during the first 1000 days from conception, are more likely to be stunted or wasted and to be disposed to infections and preventable diseases that are the direct cause of mortality for children under 5 years of age (Bryce et al., 2008). As adults, these children are more likely to have lower levels of education and employment opportunities, earn less, have larger families, provide poor care for their children, and therefore perpetuate inter-generational poverty (Bhutta et al., 2008). Similarly, children's exposure to adverse psycho-social environments undermines their cognitive functioning with lifelong consequences (Fox and Shonkoff, 2011). Corporal punishment, in particular, is closely associated with lower IQ measurements (Straus, 2009) and boys' exposure to violence in childhood is linked with adulthood violence and mental health problems (Corteras et al., 2011).

Such research has demonstrated that the interactions of genes and environment shape the developing brain. Although genes provide the blueprint for neural connections in the brain, these connections are reinforced by repeated environmental stimuli (NSCDC, 2005/2014). Children living in poverty are most at risk as they are more likely to experience under-nutrition and/or malnutrition, to be exposed to family hardship, stress and violence, to be subject to infectious diseases, to have access to poor private and public hygiene and sanitation, and to be exposed to environmental toxins (Hanson et al., 2013; Noble et al., 2015). In addition, the more children are exposed to prolonged adverse experiences, the greater the likelihood for developmental delays, as well as physical and mental health problems even later in adulthood (Engle et al., 2007; Walker at al., 2011). The research evidence is compelling and conclusive for arguing that 'the experiences children have early in life – and the environment in which they have them – shape their developing brain architecture and strongly affect whether they grow up to be healthy, productive members of society' (NSCDC, 2010: 1).

Early childhood care and development (ECCD) programmes are effective early interventions for minimising risk and improving children's developmental and learning outcomes with a long-lasting impact (Engle et al., 2011). Indeed, evaluations of ECCD programmes – mainly in economically developed countries but increasingly from low resource countries – have repeatedly demonstrated their multiple immediate benefits for children and also the longer-term benefits later on in adulthood. Such benefits include better literacy and maths skills, better overall educational attainment and outcomes, enhanced emotional and social skills, early identification and support for special educational needs, better attendance, retention and graduation in school, and in adulthood, better jobs, incomes and lower rates of misconduct, fighting and violent behaviours (see Papatheodorou and Wilson, 2016 for an extensive discussion).

Economists have also calculated the economic benefits accrued by ECCD programmes. These benefits have included savings, for example in welfare assistance, judicial costs, or the need for expensive intervention programmes for special education and behaviour improvement. There were also increased earnings in adulthood, for example in having better paid jobs and paying taxes. Economists have also calculated that there are high rates of return of investment made in such programmes. For example, the rate of return to investment for programmes implemented in the USA ranged from 7% (Abecedarian programme) to 10% (High Scope Perry programme) and even 18% (Chicago Parent-Child programme). In addition, the benefit-to-cost ratio of each of these programmes was 2.7:1, 7.2:1 and 6.9:2, respectively (Heckman, cited in Psacharopoulos, 2014). Furthermore, the benefit-to-cost ratio in ECCD programmes was much greater (8:1), compared with the return on investment in education in general (3:1) (Heckman, 2000). There are limited studies on the rates of return of investment in ECCD programmes in low and middle income countries, but a simulation economic analysis of existing programmes revealed that, by increasing preschool enrolment to 25% or 50%, the potential benefit-to-cost ratio ranged from 6.4:1 to 17.6:1 (Engle et al., 2011).

Although not comparable due to differences in methodology, for instance in regard to the kind of benefits measured and monetised, or the length of the follow-up period, these findings demonstrate that early childhood programmes generate benefits that outweigh their costs (Karoly et al., 2005). The benefits tend to be greater when ECCD programmes target the higher risk and most disadvantaged populations and provide direct services to children, especially the youngest groups. The quality, frequency, intensity and duration of the programmes are also critical for programme effectiveness (Engle et al., 2007).

The findings of early childhood programme evaluation, and their cost analysis, converge with the findings from neuroscience and brain development research, demonstrating that:

- the experiences that children have early in life determine their development and learning, which in turn benefit adult learning and functioning in society as well as the parenting of the next generation;
- the earlier children are exposed to rich learning experiences the better their development, learning and social skills;
- the best outcomes are for the youngest children and those living in poverty;
- the quality, duration and frequency of attendance in ECCD programmes are critical for children to reach their developmental potential.

The UNCRC – The unique and potent child of today

Whilst research findings established an economic argument, the United Nations Committee for the Rights of the Child (UNCRC) has provided a children's rights argument for developing early childhood programmes in order to ensure that the rights of children for survival and development, protection, education and participation are observed. The UNCRC recognises the responsibility of the family for observing these rights and articulates explicitly the role of the State for supporting families in doing so.

However, in the early 2000s the UNCRC was concerned that State parties had not given sufficient attention to recognising the rights of young children in their laws, policies and programmes. This led the CRC Committee to assert and re-emphasise that 'young children are holders of all rights enshrined in the Convention and that early childhood is a critical period for the realization of these rights' (UNCRC, 2006: 1). The Committee recognised that young children are social actors from the beginning of life, with particular interests, capacities, points of view, concerns and vulnerabilities, and they have particular requirements for physical and emotional nurture. The Committee encouraged State parties to address children's rights 'within a framework of laws, policies and programmes for early childhood, including a plan for implementation and independent monitoring ... ' (UNCRC, 2006: 3).

There are synergies between the economic and the children's rights arguments, as both acknowledge children's learning potential from birth, recognise the importance of early childhood services for children, emphasise the role of the family in enabling children's development and learning, accord responsibility to the State and its institutions in supporting families in doing so, and make the case for more investment in early childhood services, especially for targeted services for the most disadvantaged, vulnerable and marginalised populations.

Increase of investment in early childhood, however, brought about greater regulation regarding the quality of early childhood programmes and services, including the introduction of curricula and standards, educators' qualifications, training and working conditions, and the engagement of parents and families, as well as monitoring and evaluation (OECD, 2012). The latter increasingly has become a prominent feature in an effort to determine the quality and returns of investment in early childhood services and to enhance accountability towards taxpayers. Evaluation of early childhood services consists of three elements that should be examined in conjunction: programme/service quality, staff quality and children's assessment. The last of these, however, seems to be applicable across many countries, while the implementation of the other two is variable (OECD, 2015).

The universal normative child

Child assessment has long been debated and contested (and it is outside the purpose of this chapter to add to this debate) but it seems that it is here to stay, in one form or another. This view is supported by current developments and discussions in light of the Sustainable Development Goals, which included early childhood as a priority target in education (SDG 4.2). In order to monitor progress towards this target at a global level, two indicators that inherently require child assessment have been proposed, namely:

- 'Percentage of children under 5 years of age who are developmentally on track in health, learning and psychosocial well-being.'
- 'Participation rate in organized learning (one year before the official primary entry age.' (IAEG-SDG, 2015:13)

Furthermore, the Organisation for Economic Co-operation and Development (OECD) plans to introduce an International Assessment of Early Learning – an offspring of the PISA (Programme for International Student Assessment) – to assess the learning outcomes of 5 year-olds. The introduction of IELS is proposed in order 'to help countries improve the performance of their systems, to provide better outcomes for citizens and better value for money' (cited in Moss, 2016: n.p.).

In the English context, the EYFS refers explicitly to the importance of child assessment for measuring children's progress towards expected developmental and learning outcomes, for identifying their needs and for planning appropriate activities and support (see the case study below).

CASE STUDY 3.1   EXPLORING CHILD ASSESSMENT IN THE EARLY YEARS FOUNDATION STAGE (EYFS)

Progress check at age two:
 'When a child is aged between two and three, practitioners must review their progress, and provide parents and/or carers with a short written summary of their child's development in the prime areas. This progress check must identify the child's strengths, and any areas where the child's progress is less than expected.

(Continued)

(Continued)

If there are significant emerging concerns, or an identified special educational need or disability, practitioners should develop a targeted plan to support the child's future learning and development ... '

Assessment at the end of the EYFS:
   'In the final term of the year in which the child reaches age five, and no later than 30 June in that term, the EYFS Profile must be completed for each child. The Profile provides parents and carers, practitioners and teachers with a well-rounded picture of a child's knowledge, understanding and abilities, their progress against expected levels, and their readiness for Year 1 ...
   Each child's level of development must be assessed against the early learning goals ... Practitioners must indicate whether children are meeting expected levels of development, or if they are exceeding expected levels, or not yet reaching expected levels ('emerging'). This is the EYFS Profile.'

(Excerpts from the EYFS: DfE, 2014: 13–14)

Child assessment tools are mostly developmental in nature and content, covering a range of developmental domains and/or assessing specific areas of learning, as defined in curricula. For example, as Case Study 3.1 above illustrates, in England the Early Years Foundation Stage Profile (DfE, 2015) is used to assess children in prime and specific areas of learning, as per the statutory framework for the Early Years Foundation Stage (DfE, 2014). The prime areas of learning include the three developmental domains of communication and language development, physical development, and personal, social and emotional development, while the specific areas of learning cover literacy, mathematics, understanding of the world and expressive arts and designs.

Despite being debated and contested, developmental models are inherent in child assessment tools, portraying the image of the universal normative child, far removed from geopolitical, social-economic and cultural influences (Papatheodorou, 2010). Moss (2016) reminds and warns us that assessment and testing regimes that apply a universal framework to all countries, all services and all kinds of pedagogies imply that 'everything can be reduced to a common outcome, standard and measure ... without accommodating diversity' (Moss, 2016: n.p.).

If they are not mindful of how such tools and regimes may shape their views about and perceptions of children, there is a danger that practitioners may narrow and limit children's expectations about their potential, capacities and capabilities. The image of the potent and unique child, proclaimed in the UNCRC, might be obscured or forgotten under the pressures of child assessment against pre-defined developmental indicators.

Universal systemic responses to policy and regulatory frameworks that see children 'in the making' as tomorrow's productive citizens, may work at the expense of their 'being' today as unique and potent individuals who can exercise their agency and self-determination. Such responses may shape children's contemporary experiences in their settings in a uniform manner through pedagogical practices that are indiscriminate with regard to their unique abilities and capabilities, talents, background and cultural milieu. Moreover, child assessment scores may become the yardstick for determining service quality and staff performance, independent of contextual and cultural factors, thereby influencing childhood provision.

Furthermore, the fact that early childhood programmes in particular are seen as counter-balancing poor home circumstances at the beginning of children's lives, leads to their becoming a high equity priority for policy makers (OECD, 2008). As a result, the attention of policy makers has shifted from universal provision towards targeted services, especially for children experiencing disadvantage, poverty, specific vulnerabilities and/or marginalisation, in order to reduce inequality.

The focus on targeted services denotes a change of direction and course of action in the field. Early childhood is increasingly seen as – and has become – an interventionist service. The assessment requirements in the case study above illustrate this; the requirement that a targeted plan is developed for 2 year-olds, whose progress is checked against prime areas of learning, raises significant concerns. Despite its noble cause, this requirement is not without its challenges. There is a danger that interventionist early childhood provision is forcing and morphing young children into a universal prototype, as defined by intended learning outcomes, child assessment norms and quality indicators. The uniqueness and individuality of children, and the proclaimed respect for difference and diversity involving the unique and potent individual child, may be threatened and sacrificed in interventionist services with great personal, social and cultural cost, including unforeseen consequences in the long run.

It is therefore important for educators to be mindful of the inherent image of the child portrayed through assessment tools and monitoring systems, and how these may – wittingly or unwittingly – impact on their pedagogical practices.

CASE STUDY 3.2   EXPLORING PEDAGOGICAL PRAXIS – KEEPING SIGHT OF THE UNIQUE AND POTENT CHILD

Annie is attending the reception class. Born in September, she is one of the older children in the class. According to her teacher Annie is content, well-behaved and mature for her age. She started school well, but three months into the school year she started complaining to her mother that school is boring and she does not get time to work or play with her friends. This came to a head when she refused to go to school.

It took some time for her mother to find out the real reason for Annie's refusal to go to school. Annie explained that when she is 'doing her numbers' she finishes her work before all the other children in her group. So sometimes she had to wait for them to finish but it was difficult to keep quiet. The teacher would then ask her to choose another activity for herself but it was not fun playing on her own.

(Continued)

(Continued)

Annie's mother spoke to the teacher about the situation. The teacher was surprised about this. She acknowledged that Annie was good at maths and was even exceeding expectations in this area for her age. Annie was quick to understand what was expected in the activities that her group was doing and she often finished before all the other children. It was for this reason the teacher suggested that she could choose to do something else.

Reflecting on the situation and after discussions with Annie and her mother, the teacher decided to give Annie additional work that was above the expected level that her group was working at. In this way, she would work on her level of understanding while she remained in the group. This change seemed to work well.

The case study above demonstrates the way expected outcomes and assessment influence the planning and organisation of learning activities. The teacher's language about Annie's achievement (e.g. being in the *top group* and *exceeding* expectation) shows that the organisation and planning of group activities were based on the expected levels of achievement as defined in the EYFS profile. However, this level of work was still below Annie's actual abilities and she was quick to finish the given tasks and activities. Initially, Annie was able to self-regulate herself and keep quiet after she finished her work in order to remain in the group. With time, however, she became frustrated and stressed; she started telling children what they had to do and rushed them to finish. It was at this time when the teacher would ask her to choose another activity for herself. Yet this was equally frustrating for Annie, as she was separated from the other children.

The case study also illustrates the potential challenges teachers experience when they plan and organise learning with expected learning outcomes in mind and possible unintended and unforeseen consequences for children. Whilst children may need support to achieve the expected level of achievement against expected learning outcomes, this may not always enable each and every child to fully develop their full potential. Clearly, Annie's teacher planned the learning activities in line with what Annie *ought to be doing* with regard to what was already *known* (e.g. curricula, standards and expected learning outcomes, including extant knowledge in the field, and the skills and competencies required for working with young children). It was, however, her awareness of Annie's challenges and her own open-minded and reflective attitude that enabled her to consider and find out what was *possible to be done* by *knowing* the individual child and her level of understanding and abilities.

Setting out standards and expected learning outcomes may be desirable for policy makers who aim at ensuring that all children have equal opportunities for reaching a certain level of development and learning. The aim of educational policy is to ensure that educational provision is *just*. The drawback of such policies is the underlying assumption that all children start from an equal basis and will reach the same pre-defined outcomes. This has been well illustrated in the case study above and it will now be briefly discussed in the context of equity in education.

Equity in education is understood as minimum standards for all or equal outcomes for all regardless of social and family circumstances (PPI, 2011). Other definitions highlight the two-dimensional nature of equity. For example, the OECD (2008) defines equity in terms of fairness and inclusion while UNICEF (2015) sees equity in terms of access to and quality of education. Equity in terms of inclusion and quality requires the existence of, and adherence to, minimum standards for achieving certain outcomes, regardless of individual children's personal and social background and capital. Equity in terms of access and fairness – to recall Brown (cited in Wood et al., 2011) – denotes unequal treatment of those who are not equal, in order to minimise inequality.

The conceptualisation and definitions of equity shed light on the fact that not every child starts from an equal basis. Therefore while universal standards and learning outcomes ensure a just educational system, they may be limiting in scope and purpose if an individual child's circumstances and potential are not considered. It is then crucial for educators to keep in mind that working with children is not just about adherence to policy requirements or the application of technical skills and/or extant knowledge in the field. It is also about making sound judgements for selecting and employing appropriate and relevant extant knowledge and skills to meet the needs of individual children and address their particular personal and social circumstances, whilst at the same time operating within existing policy frameworks and requirements. It is about being fair to individual children by ensuring different treatment to level their learning opportunities.

Equity in education then is about being both just and fair – just by setting out standards and expected learning outcomes that determine what ought to be done on the basis of what is already known, fair by requiring educators to make sound pedagogical judgements to determine what can possibly be done by knowing and considering individual children. Being just requires conformity with policy, while being fair entails moral judgements regarding what is good for individual children.

Being just and fair, however, is not a straightforward or unproblematic concept, for it is important that each is exercised without external interference, self-interest or favouritism. Thus the balancing of what ought to be done on the basis of what is already known, and what is possible to be done by knowing individual children highlights the ethical dimension of the educators' pedagogical practice. As a result, pedagogical practice inherits educators' personal and professional responsibility for being informed and informing, for examining dominant biases and prevailing values and beliefs, for moving beyond a technical and skills-oriented education that supports certain valued skills, and for espousing the potent, unique and capable individual children who are valued and enabled to exercise their agency for matters that affect their lives.

Annie's case (above) illustrates that teachers need to be reflective in following policy requirements while they remain alert to individual children's learning. For it is crucial that they encourage and nurture children's individuality, uniqueness and potential, whilst at the same time pursuing universal learning outcomes for all.

QUESTIONS FOR REFLECTION

1. Reflecting on Annie's situation in Case Study 3.2, why do you think the teacher organised the learning activities the way she did? What are the challenges in planning learning activities for all and each individual child, whilst working within existing policies and regulatory frameworks?

2. To what extent and in what ways do policy and regulatory frameworks influence pedagogical praxis, and what are the common dilemmas experienced by practitioners?

3. What are the potential advantages and disadvantages of making judgements of children's progress against the proposed categories (i.e. exceeding, meeting and not yet reaching expected outcomes)?

4. What are your views regarding targeted versus universal services for children? You may like to consider the UNCRC and current policy developments.

5. To what extent and how do you promote justice and fairness for all and each child? List and describe some concrete actions and strategies.

SUMMARY

Research evidence and the UNCRC have brought childhood, particularly early childhood, to the forefront of national and international policies and have been instrumental in increasing government investment for services. Inevitably this has led to the introduction of greater regulation, followed by child assessment, monitoring and evaluation in order to establish quality of services and the returns of investment. Despite being debated and highly contested, child assessment is now widely used to determine the quality of childhood services. This, however, is not without its challenges. Child assessment tools are largely developmental in nature, portraying a universal normative child, far removed from their context and cultural milieu. It is therefore important for educators to be aware of how policies and assessment tools might influence and shape their pedagogical praxis to form and mould the child. Whilst educators are expected to frame their pedagogical praxis within existing policies and regulatory frameworks, they should also be mindful that they carry an ethical responsibility for making judgements and pedagogical choices to ensure that each and every child is treated as a unique and potent individual.

End of chapter glossary

- **Children's rights** are the human rights afforded to children with special attention paid to their protection, provision and participation.
- **Early Childhood Care and Development** (ECCD) **programmes** are early intervention programmes designed to minimise risk and improve children's lives and circumstances.

- **Universal experience of childhood** refers to the notion that all children experience childhood in the same way, regardless of their particular circumstances and context, and their social, historical and cultural milieu.
- **Regulation of childhood programmes and services** involves the setting out, monitoring and evaluation of curricula, standards, conditions and expected outcomes for children attending early childhood services.

Further reading

Papatheodorou, T. (2010) Being, belonging and becoming: some worldviews of early childhood in contemporary curricula, *Forum on Public Policy Online*, 2.

Psacharopoulos, G. (2014) Benefit and Costs of Education Targets for the Post-2015 Development Agenda: Post-2015 Consensus, Education Assessment Papers. Working Paper as of 17 July 2014. Copenhagen Consensus Centre. Available at www.copen hagenconsensus.com/sites/default/files/education_assessment_-_psacharopoulos_0. pdf (last accessed 12 September 2016).

References

Bhutta, Z.A., Ahmed, T., Black, R.E., Cousens, S., Dewey, K., Giugliani, E., Haider, B.A., Kirkwood, B., Morris, S.S., Sachdev, H.P.S., Shekar, M. and the Maternal and Child Undernutrition Study Group (2008) What works? Interventions for maternal and child undernutrition and survival, *The Lancet*, 371 (9610): 417–440.

Bryce, J., Coitinho, D., Darnton-Hill, I., Pellerier, D., Pinstru-Andersen, P. and the Maternal and Child Undernutrition Study Group (2008) Maternal and child undernutrition: effective action at national level, *The Lancet*, 371 (9611): 510–526.

Corteras, M., Singh, A., Heilman, B., Barker, G. and Verma, R. (2011) 'Analysing Data from the International Men and Gender Equality Survey (IMAGES): Connections between Early Childhood Experience of Violence and Intimate Partner Violence'. In B. van Leer Foundation (ed.), *Hidden Violence: Protecting Young Children at Home. Early Childhood Matters*, 116: 26–31.

Department for Education (DfE) (2014) Statutory Framework for the Early Years Foundation Stage: Setting the Standards for Learning, Development and Care for Children from Birth to Five. Available at www.gov.uk/government/uploads/system/uploads/attachment_data/file/335504/EYFS_framework_from_1_September_2014__with_clarification_note.pdf (last accessed 19 September 2016).

Department for Education (DfE) (2015) *Early Years Foundation Stage Profile 2016 Handbook*. Standards and Testing Agency. Available at www.gov.uk/government/uploads/system/uploads/attachment_data/file/488745/EYFS_handbook_2016_-_FINAL.pdf (last accessed 19 September 2016).

Engle, P.L., Black, M.M., Behrman, J.R., Cabral de Mello, M., Gertler, P.J., Kapiriri, L., Martorell, R. and Yong, M.E. (2007) Strategies to avoid the loss of developmental potential in more than 200 million children in the developing world, *The Lancet*, 369 (9557): 229–242.

Engle, P.L., Fernald, L.C.H., Alderman, H., Behrman, J., O'Gara, C., Yousafzai, A., Cabral de Mello, M., Hidrobo, M., Ulkuer, N., Ertem, I., Iltus, S. and the Global Child Development Steering Group (2011) Strategies for reducing inequalities and improving developmental outcomes for young children in low-income and middle-income countries, *The Lancet*, 378: 1339–1353.

Fox, N.A and Shonkoff, J.P. (2011) 'Violence and Development: How Persistence, Fear and Anxiety can Affect Young Children's Learning and Behaviour and Health'. In B. van Leer

Foundation (ed.), *Early Childhood Matters, Hidden Violence: Protecting Young Children at Home*, 116: 8–14. Available at http://46y5eh11fhgw3ve3ytpwxt9r.wpengine.netdna-cdn.com/wp-content/uploads/2016/05/Early-Childhood-Matters_How-persistent-fear-and-anxiety-can-affect-young-childrens-health.pdf (last accessed 19 September 2016).

Hanson, J.L., Hair, N., Shen, D.G., Shi, F., Gilmore, J.H. and Wolfe, B.L. (2013) Family poverty affects the rate of human infant brain growth, *PLoS ONE*, 8 (12): e80954. doi:10.1371/journal.pone.0080954. Available at http://journals.plos.org/plosone/article?id=10.1371/journal.pone.0080954#pone.0080954-United1 (last accessed 1 September 2016).

Heckman, J.J. (2000) *Policies to Foster Human Capital*. Joint Center for Poverty Research, Working Paper 154. Chicago: Northwestern University/University of Chicago.

IAEG-SDG (2015) *Results of the List of Indicators Reviewed at the Second IAEG-SDG Meeting*. Available at http://unstats.un.org/sdgs/files/meetings/iaeg-sdgs-meeting-02/Outcomes/Agenda%20Item%204%20-20Review%20of%20proposed%20indicators%20-%202%20Nov%202015.pdf (last accessed 19 September 2016).

Karoly, L.A., Kilburn, M.R. and Cannon, J.S. (2005) *Early Childhood Interventions Proven Results*. California: RAND.

Moss, P. (2016) Is a preschool PISA what we want for our young children? Available at https://ioelondonblog.wordpress.com/2016/08/08/is-a-preschool-pisa-what-we-want-for-our-young-children/ (last accessed 20 September 2016).

National Scientific Council on the Developing Child (NSCDC) (2005/2014) *Excessive Stress Disrupts the Architecture of the Developing Brain: Working Paper No. 3*. Updated Edition. Available at www.developingchild.harvard.edu (last accessed 20 September 2016).

National Scientific Council on the Developing Child (NSCDC) (2010) *Early Experiences Can Alter Gene Expression and Affect Long-Term Development: Working Paper No. 10*. Available at http://developingchild.harvard.edu/index.php/resources/reports_and_working_papers/working_papers/wp10 (last accessed 31 August 2016).

Noble, K.G., Houston, S.M., Brito, N.H. et al. (2015) Family income, parental education and brain structure in children and adolescents, *Nat Neurosci.*, 18 (5):773–778. doi: 10.1038/nn.3983.

OECD (2008) *Ten Steps to Equity in Education*. Available at www.oecd.org/education/school/39989494.pdf (last accessed 21 October 2016).

OECD (2012) *Starting Strong III – A Quality Toolbox for Early Childhood Education and Care, Executive Summary*. Available at www.oecd.org/edu/school/49325825.pdf (last accessed 19 September 2016).

OECD (2015) *Starting Strong IV: Monitoring Quality in Early Childhood Education and Care*. Available at www.keepeek.com/Digital-Asset-Management/oecd/education/starting-strong-iv_9789264233515-en#page1 (last accessed 19 September 2016).

Papatheodorou, T. (2010) 'Being, belonging and becoming: some worldviews of early childhood in contemporary curricula', *Forum on Public Policy Online*, 2.

Papatheodorou, T. and Wilson, M. (2016) 'The International Perspective on Early Childhood Education'. In I. Palaiologou (ed.), *The Early Years Foundation Stage: Theory and Practice* (3rd edition). London: Sage.

PPI (2011) *Issues Paper 1: Equity and Education*. Prepared by the Public Policy Institute of Australian Catholic University for the Independent Schools Council of Australia. Available at http://isca.edu.au/wp-content/uploads/2011/03/PPI-Paper-1-Equity-and-Education.pdf (last accessed 8 December 2016).

Psacharopoulos, G. (2014) *Benefit and Costs of Education Targets for the Post-2015 Development Agenda: Post-2015 Consensus, Education Assessment Papers*. Working Paper as of 17 July 2014. Copenhagen Consensus Centre. Available at www.copenhagen

consensus.com/sites/default/files/education_assessment_-_psacharopoulos_0.pdf (last accessed 12 September 2016).

Straus, M.A. (2009) 'Differences in corporal punishment by parents in 32 nations and its relation to national differences'. IQ Paper presented at the 14th International Conference on Violence, Abuse and Trauma, 25 September, San Diego, California. Available at http://pubpages.unh.edu/~mas2/CP-empirical.htm (last accessed 24 March 2016).

UNCRC (1989) *United Nations Convention on the Rights of the Child*. (Adopted and opened for signature, ratification and accession by General Assembly Resolution 44/25 of 20 November 1989. Entry into force 2 September 1990. In accordance with Article 49.) Available at www.unicef.org.uk/Documents/Publication-pdfs/UNCRC_PRESS2009 10web.pdf (last accessed 15 September 2016).

UNCRC (2006) Implementing Child Rights in Early Childhood. Committee on the Rights of the Child, Fortieth Session, Geneva, 12–30 September 2005. Available at www2.ohchr. org/english/bodies/crc/docs/AdvanceVersions/GeneralComment7Rev1.pdf (last accessed 19 September 2016).

UNESCO (1990) *World Declaration on Education for All and Framework for Action to Meet Basic Learning Needs* (adopted by the World Conference on Education for All: Meeting Basic Learning Needs, Jomtien, Thailand, 5–9 March). Paris: UNESCO.

UNESCO (2000) *World Education Forum: The Dakar Framework for Action, Education for All: Meeting our Collective Commitments* (adopted by the World Education Forum 26–28 March). Paris: UNESCO.

UNESCO (2010) *Moscow Framework for Action and Cooperation: Harnessing the Wealth of Nations.* World Conference on Early Childhood Care and Education, Building the Wealth of Nations, 27–29 September, Moscow, Russian Federation. Available at http://unesdoc. unesco.org/images/0018/001898/189882e.pdf (last accessed 15 September 2016).

UNICEF (2015) *For Every Child, A Fair Chance: The Promise of Equity*. New York: UNICEF.

United Nations (UN) (2015) *Transforming our World: The 2030 Agenda for Sustainable Development*. A/RES/70/1. Available at https://sustainabledevelopment.un.org/content/documents/21252030%20Agenda%20for%20Sustainable%20Development%20web. pdf (last accessed 23 August 2016).

Walker, S.P., Wachs, T.D., Grantham-McGregor, S., Black, M.M., Nelson, C.A., Huffman, S.L., Baker-Henningham, H., Chang, S.M., Hamadani, J.D., Lozoff, B., Meeks Gardner, J.M., Powell, C.A., Rahman, A. and Richter, L. (2011) Inequality in early childhood: risk and protective factors for early child development, *The Lancet*, 378: 1325–1338.

Wood, E., Levinson, M., Postlethwaite, K. and Black, A. (2011) *Equity Matters*. Exeter: University of Exeter, Education International Research Institute.

4

THE SEN/D CHILD

MARIE CASLIN

CHAPTER OBJECTIVES

- To understand that 'SEN/D' is historically, socially and culturally constructed.
- To gain an appreciation for what the field of disability studies can bring to our understanding of the educational experiences of disabled children.
- To offer an alternative approach to educating all children which celebrates diversity.

This chapter will illustrate that 'SEN/D' is historically, socially and culturally constructed. The starting position is that no child 'has' Special Educational Needs (SEN). Although some children will experience impairment, their educational needs are made 'special' as a result of the ways in which we conceptualise and organise our education systems (Terzi, 2005; Penketh, 2014). Having worked with young people who have been labelled as having 'behavioural problems', I have gained first-hand experience of the impact our current education system has on the experiences of disabled children. Throughout this chapter I will be drawing on examples from my research, to illustrate the problematic nature of the term SEN/D. The chapter seeks to demonstrate that instead of focusing on what is 'wrong' with disabled children, we should be critically examining our social environment and how this in many ways creates disability. In order to do this, the field of disability studies will be drawn from. Within this academic field of study the voice of the disabled child should take priority, whereas within other academic fields including psychology, medicine and education it is often the professional's voice that dominates. With this in mind, throughout the chapter the disabled child will be referred to, to further reflect the position that SEN/D is not something an individual child has but is a reflection of how our society creates SEN/D by not celebrating natural human variation. To start though, in order to gain an understanding of how disabled children experience the world today, we have to look back at our history.

Historical influences on the position of the disabled child

For the purposes of this chapter there is a focus on two key historical events to illustrate the impact our history has had on how we view disabled childhoods today. Firstly, when reviewing the literature surrounding disabled childhoods, the Ancient Greeks are often seen as having a significant impact on our response to the disabled child (Priestley, 2003). During this time infanticide – the killing of an infant – was a common practice. Garland (1995) draws our attention to a reflection on the established Greek practice, which can be found in a section entitled 'How to recognise that it is worth raising' in *Gynaecology*, written by a Greek physician, Soranos, in the second century AD. It states that the child:

> ... should be perfect in all its parts, limbs and senses, and have passages that are not obstructed, including the ears, nose, throat, urethra and anus. Its natural movements be neither slow nor feeble, its limbs bend and stretch, its size and shape should be appropriate, and it should respond to natural stimuli. (Garland, 1995:14)

It is here that we see the introduction of ideas around there being a 'perfect' child; this led to a child with any form of impairment being considered undesirable and in extreme cases killed. Although infanticide is no longer common practice, this fascination with bodily perfection continues to be a feature of modern-day society. You only have to pick up a magazine or turn on the TV to witness how this still impacts on our ideas of what bodies can and should do (Garland-Thomson, 1997). The media have been heavily criticised for promoting certain images of how bodies should be and negatively portraying those who do not conform to this very narrow image (Cameron, 2014). These ideas will then be reflected in social encounters and can have a potentially damaging effect on how children see themselves (Bolt, 2012).

The second period of history I would like to focus on is industrialisation. For many academics the advent of industrialisation is seen as having a key influence on the lives of disabled children, as it is here that we really see the growth of the medical profession and its influence on disabled children's lives (Barnes, 1997). Prior to this, disabled children would have been the responsibility of the family. As we had a largely agrarian society, education was not needed to facilitate inclusion (Hodkinson, 2016). During this period, we also see the emergence of the medicalisation of the body and the mind (Barnes, 1997). Oliver (1990) argues this led to disabled people beginning to be perceived as a social problem as they were deemed to be a potential drain on social welfare. Individuals began to be judged on what they could contribute to the mode of production and their financial worth; those who could not contribute became a problem (Oliver, 1990). This led to ideas around eugenics becoming popularised. The term 'eugenics' means to be well born and refers in particular to philosophies for selecting the characteristics of people in a population; specifically deciding who should be born, who should die, and who should reproduce (Priestley, 2003). With the rise of scientific rationalism and medical knowledge, attention turned increasingly to the possibility of correction and cure, with emphasis being placed on a desire to resolve or eliminate impairment characteristics within children (Priestley, 2003). Worryingly, these ideas continue to have an influence on modern medicine. There have been many advances in medical knowledge and technology, which have focused on identifying potential birth defects. Indeed, recently the National Screening Committee approved a simple test for identifying Down's Syndrome whilst the foetus is still in the womb. Statistics suggest that around 90% of pregnancies that involve the 'condition' end in termination. In 2014, 693 abortions were carried out for this reason – a significant rise of 34% since 2011 (Stanley, 2016). The fact that the number of terminations appears to be increasing is of concern as it suggests that the lives of disabled children are not seen as being as valuable as 'normal' children. This further reflects society's continued focus on producing 'perfect' children.

However, in recent times we have seen challenges from disabled people to this problematic view of impairment. In the United Kingdom, the disabled people's movement was the force behind the reclaiming of the term 'disability' from professionals in medicine and social care (UPIAS, 1976; Cameron, 2014). At this time, for disabled people, there were two different approaches to viewing and understanding their position within society. Firstly, the medical model which, as illustrated above, was clearly dominant throughout disability history, in which the emphasis is placed on cure and intervention (identifying what is 'wrong' with the individual and finding ways to 'fix' them). However, secondly the Union of the Physically Impaired Against Segregation (UPIAS) developed an alternative to the medical model, which has become known as the social model of disability (Barnes, 1997). Here the emphasis is moved away from the individual and instead placed on societal structures and how they can be seen to create disability. Disabled children then do not have a disability, they may have an impairment such as visual impairment or physical impairment, but what disables them is how society responds to their differences. For UPIAS there is a clear distinction between having an impairment and being disabled. This is summed up with the following definitions:

> **Impairment:** lacking part of or all of a limb, or having a defective limb, organ or mechanism of the body.

> **Disability:** the disadvantage or restriction of activity caused by a contemporary social organisation which takes no or little account of people who have physical impairments and thus excludes them from participation in the mainstream of social activities. (UPIAS, 1976: 14).

There have been criticisms that disabled children have been noticeably absent in the advances of the social model of disability (Connors and Stalker, 2007). Due to disabled children being negatively stereotyped as 'passive, vulnerable and dependent' (Davis and Watson, 2002:159), they have been seen as problematic to researchers and policy makers. However, Connors and Stalker argue the problems of a disabled childhood are a result of 'social relations, cultural representations and behaviour of adults' (2007: 22). The voice of the disabled child will only be

Table 4.1 Summary of the models of disability

Medical Model	Social Model
Blame is placed on the individual child	Blame is placed on societal structures surrounding the child
Focus is placed on assessment, intervention and cure	Focus is placed on ensuring the child has a say on what interventions are available
Individual child needs to change to fit into society	Society needs to change to accommodate diversity
Professionals' voice dominates – child's voice is silenced	Voice of the disabled child is heard
Segregated education system	Inclusive education system
Labelling and ability-grouping	Acknowledge and celebrate natural human variation

heard if the adults surrounding them are willing to listen. The publication of Article 12 of the *United Nations Convention on the Rights of the Child* (UNCRC) in 1989 was seen as a key development in advocating the voice of the child. This article stated that:

> Parties shall assure to the child who is capable of forming his or her own views the right to express those views freely, in all matters affecting the child, the views of the child being given due weight in accordance with the age and maturity of the child. (UN General Assembly, 1989: 12)

Despite the introduction of the Convention, doubts have been raised as to whether adults are actually willing to embrace the concept of voice (Coad and Lewis, 2004). Furthermore, the application of these articles will be based on adults' subjective judgements, not least in that the application of such articles would be largely dependent on adult interpretations. For instance, they will be responsible for determining who is deemed 'capable and mature'. This leads to questions as to whether disabled children will be considered capable and mature. Alongside these concerns it appears that children themselves had very little input into the construction of the Convention (Hill and Tisdall, 1997). Even within more recent government legislation, such as the new SEN Code of Practice (DfE and DoH, 2015), they draw on the language used within the UNCRC stating children's views should be given 'due weight according to their age, maturity and capability' (2015: 20). Currently then it would seem that disabled children are being denied their right to participate in decisions regarding their education, as adults continue to determine who is worthy of a voice. Yet there is a significant amount of evidence to suggest that disabled children have important messages to share (O'Connor et al., 2011).

Despite these concerns there is no doubt the disabled people's movement has been extremely influential in calling for a change in how society responds to and treats disabled people. The social model highlights that the biggest obstacle to disabled children's meaningful inclusion into mainstream community life is negative public attitudes (Barnes, 1997). The importance of social attitudes should not be underestimated. Over the last couple of decades lots of attention has been paid to the oppression experienced by other social groups, however for many working within the field of disability studies disabled people continue to be ignored. As we strive to be a more equal society, unfortunately evidence suggests that disabled children are still likely to encounter oppression. A recent study commissioned by the Equality and Human Rights Commission (2015) focused on whether Britain is now a fairer society; the study found that disabled children are more likely to be excluded from school, the attainment gap between disabled children and their non-disabled peers has widened, and disabled young people are less likely to be in further education, employment or training.

Whilst there can be no doubt that the position of disabled children has improved (for example children are no longer placed in institutions and many disabled children are now living longer due to advances in medical practice), there are still several reasons to query the social position of disabled children (McLaughlin et al., 2016). The chapter will now be divided into two sections to critically explore the impact the two models of disability continue to have on the lives of disabled children, focusing specifically on their educational experiences.

The medical model

As mentioned earlier in the chapter, industrialisation played a key role in determining the position of disabled children. With these changes individuals began to be viewed in terms of what they could contribute to society and were judged on productivity (Oliver, 1990). With the roles of children changing and largely being determined by what they could offer to wider society, we saw the first attempts to educate all children. Unfortunately it did not take long for some children to start to become segregated and excluded as they began to be viewed as a 'social burden' (Tomlinson, 2012). It is here that we see the introduction of special education. For some, special educational provision was brought about by a desire to promote the well-being of mankind and was motivated by individual charitable acts; this has been referred to as benevolent humanitarianism (Hodkinson, 2016). Tomlinson, however, would refute this notion, instead suggesting that there are only certain groups within society that will benefit from a segregated education system:

> Special schools develop because it is in the interests of particular groups in a society that they should develop, and that they should develop in particular ways ... the forms that special education have taken in the past and today are the products of particular vested interests in society. (2012: 27)

For Tomlinson (2012) then the history of special education must be viewed in terms of the benefits it brought for a developing industrial society. Clearly, there are particular groups and professionals within society who have a vested interest in the continued categorisation and medicalisation of children.

Normalising childhood

Within our society we, as individuals, continually compare ourselves to each other and this starts as soon as a child is born:

> We live in a world of norms. Each of us endeavours to be normal or else deliberately tries to avoid that state. We consider what the average person does, thinks, earns, or consumes. We rank our intelligence, our cholesterol level, our weight, height, sex drive, bodily dimensions along some conceptual line from subnormal to above-average … Our children are ranked in school and tested to determine where they fit into a normal curve of learning, of intelligence. (Davis, 2013: 1)

Schools play a vital role in monitoring a child's development. Upon entering school children will be assessed and placed into different groups based on their perceived ability. Within education children may fall into one of the following categories: high ability, average ability, low ability and SEN/D. Once a child has been categorised it is likely this label will stay with them throughout their educational journey and shape how they are perceived by adults and peers (Boaler et al., 2000). This is clearly a cause for concern, especially for disabled children as research also suggests that teachers will have lower expectations of those labelled as having SEN/D (Boaler et al., 2000). Within current government documentation there continues to be an emphasis on comparing children based on their perceived abilities, with the most recent SEN Code of Practice stating:

> A child of compulsory school age or a young person has a learning difficulty or disability if he or she:
>
> - has a significantly greater difficulty in learning than the majority of others of the same age; or
> - has a disability which prevents or hinders him or her from making use of facilities of a kind generally provided for others of the same age in mainstream schools or mainstream post-16 institutions. (DfE and DoH, 2015: 15–16)

Close examination of these policies, and the language used within, further reinforces the idea that it is the child who is at fault. Evidence from research suggests that such government policies continue to serve to 'other' disabled children as they do not conform to our expectations in terms of how children should be within an educational setting (Bolt, 2012; Penketh, 2014). The use of the term 'other' here refers to how the language we use to describe disabled children leads to this group of children being seen as somehow different from their peers, creating a binary of them and us. The focus is placed on 'fixing' the pupil to fit in with the expected educational norms.

Medicalising childhood

One of the most controversial labels that will come under the SEN/D umbrella is Attention Deficit Hyperactivity Disorder (ADHD). Having completed a research study that sought to explore the educational experiences of children identified as having 'behavioural problems' enabled me to gain an understanding of how children see themselves within the confines of education. These young people will then have a variety of labels attached to them including ADHD. Here, blame for behaviour is placed on the individual as they become defined by and reduced to the label that has been attached to them (Garland-Thomson, 1997; Bolt, 2012). The strategies employed have tended to focus on 'treating' the pupil to modify their behaviour (Coppock, 2002; Timimi, 2009). Indeed, in recent years, we have seen a dramatic increase in the number of young people being prescribed medication as a method of controlling their behaviour (Timimi, 2009; Smith, 2012). As part of the study the young people were asked to reflect on their experiences in education. In the following case study Clare provides an insight into the impact being prescribed Ritalin had on her classroom encounters.

CASE STUDY 4.1   EXPLORING CLARE'S EXPERIENCE

Clare was only 5 years-old when she was first diagnosed with ADHD. When speaking to Clare about her educational experiences she appeared unhappy in school and she described numerous occasions where she would make the decision to remove herself. Clare had experienced difficult relationships with teachers whom she felt would treat her differently due to her 'condition'. She experienced difficulties when first taking her medication as she struggled to swallow her pills:

> I went the doctor's because my mum thought this is not right for a kid to just run round and hit people and scream at teachers. They did a test and said she has got ADHD, me mum was like oh right, so they gave me medicine and then I took that but it was dead horrible. I tried not to take it but my mum used to force it down my throat. (Clare)

During her time in education she feels she would be treated differently to her peers due to her ADHD diagnosis and this had a negative impact on her relationships with other pupils:

> One of the kids would say that is not fair she goes out half of the lesson and the teacher would be like well you haven't got ADHD, so it is not fair on the other kids but it is not my fault. (Clare)

For Clare, being prescribed medication had a significant impact on her educational experiences. She was all too aware of the stigma that is attached to the ADHD label and felt having this label would shape how both teachers and peers responded to her.

It has been suggested that the short-term improvements in pupil behaviour as a result of medication are more likely to be beneficial to parents and teachers rather than to the young people themselves (Cantwell, 1999; Miller and Leger, 2003). The findings from my study would support these claims with the processes of labelling, assessing and medicalising pupils being perceived as a priority for adults.

The social model

Throughout this next section of the chapter the intention is to demonstrate that it is the structures and organisation of our education system that create the need for the SEN/D label. This will be achieved by drawing on ideas from the social model of disability to explore some of the systematic and attitudinal barriers that have led to the segregation and exclusion of disabled children. For many working in the field of disability studies it is often understood that this is caused by the school's failure to take into account children's diversity in learning styles. It is widely acknowledged that, due to the pressure exerted on schools, they focus on attainment and this leaves little room for those working with children to develop creative approaches to ensure children are fulfilling their potential (Goodley, 2011; Drummond and Hart with Swann, 2013).

Systematic barriers

Throughout recent educational history there have been attempts to try to make our education system more inclusive and accepting of difference. Despite the notion of inclusion being a feature of the education system for over forty years, these young people remain on the periphery of mainstream schooling (Caslin, 2014). This is to some extent due to government policies being laden with contradictions between inclusion and exclusion (Tomlinson, 2012; Hodkinson, 2016). On the one hand, schools are expected to be able to support disabled children, and on the other, teachers face pressure to raise attainment. This has meant that for some children it can be extremely difficult, if not impossible, to find suitable educational provision. Our current education system simply does not work for some children and this leads to them being removed from educational environments. The difficulties experienced by some children in finding suitable educational provision are summed up in the case study below.

CASE STUDY 4.2   EXPLORING WHITNEY-BOB'S EXPERIENCE

Whitney-Bob was attending an alternative female provision and was described as experiencing Behavioural, Emotional and Social Difficulties (BESD). She had been excluded from school numerous times. This meant that throughout her educational journey she had experienced a wide range of provisions, including mainstream,

(Continued)

(Continued)

support centres and colleges of further education. Whitney-Bob was living with her nan as her mother had passed away when she was only 4 years-old. She states that she managed to cope in primary school, however she started to display 'challenging' behaviour in secondary school. She believes that this was due to her 'getting in with the wrong crowd'. She described the difficulties she experienced maintaining her educational placements as she would only manage to remain in provisions for short periods of time:

> It isn't that I don't like the teachers, it is just too big and too many people. I don't like being with loads of people, it may sound stupid because if I go out I will be with loads of people, I just don't like being with people I don't know. (Whitney-Bob)

Despite not having an officially recognised medical diagnosis Whitney-Bob expressed feeling different from her peers:

> I can't help it. I am weird, one minute I am nice then the next minute I am horrible and the next minute I want to cry, then I want to go mad, I think I have got something wrong with me. (Whitney-Bob)

Adults surrounding Whitney-Bob were becoming increasingly concerned about what impact her chaotic educational journey would have on her future prospects:

> I mean, she is going to find it hard to get into college when she wants to go. When she really comes round to what she wants to do it may be too late because they won't entertain it, because let's face it if you were in college and there was a girl like Whitney-Bob who didn't go in and you kept her place open you would go mad. I told them why keep her place open if she is not coming in, it is not fair on other kids that want to go and she can't see the logic in that. (Whitney-Bob's nan)

The above case study highlights the difficulties educational professionals face in terms of identifying suitable educational placements for disabled children. Although disabled children will be educated in a variety of different settings, the number attending maintained special schools has gradually increased from 38.2% in 2010 to 42.9% in 2016 (DfE, 2016). This suggests that disabled children are still being segregated from their peers and that schools, rather than embracing diversity, continue to remove children who do not conform to their expectations of how bodies and minds should be (Tomlinson, 2012). The case study also highlights the difficulties in identifying SEN/D and how labels can be attached to children that will then shape not only how adults perceive them, but also how they perceive themselves. Labels appear to be something of a double-edged sword: children require the label in order to access specialist support, but once they have obtained it this can have a detrimental impact on the individual child's educational experiences (Caslin, 2014). With research indicating that disabled children are less likely to achieve

GCSEs or go to university, having this label will have significant implications on a child's future outcomes (Equality and Human Rights Commission, 2015). There is increasing pressure placed on children to conform, so when they feel like they are not meeting our expectations of how children should be in school they feel there must be something wrong with them.

Attitudinal barriers

For those working in the field of disability studies, as highlighted earlier in the chapter, the biggest barrier to achieving the meaningful inclusion of all children is social attitudes (Barnes, 1997; Bolt, 2012; Caslin, 2014). Here the role of teachers is obviously significant. Those working in the teaching profession continue to argue that they have not received adequate training to enable them to support disabled children (Penketh and Waite, 2015). Penketh and Waite have raised concerns regarding the continuous emphasis placed on training, stating that 'many educators continue to have the misconception that to teach disabled children successfully lots of "facts" about impairment are necessary ... Educators under this misapprehension enrol on various "training" courses in the hope that they will acquire the "special knowledge"' (2015: 75). Worryingly, this can lead to the 'othering' of disabled children as teachers may start to feel they are not equipped to support all children, when in reality:

> Children who are slower to learn – for whatever reason – need the same in order to learn as any other child. They need the kind of things which our humanity tells us they need: interest, confidence, freedom from worry, a warm and patient teacher. (Thomas and Loxley, 2007: 27)

Clearly a cultural and structural change is needed. We need to move away from our focus on assessing and identifying needs to empower teachers and practitioners to support all children. It can be hard to imagine a school where attainment is not the main priority, yet there are examples of schools who have successfully moved away from this approach. In a project entitled 'Learning without Limits' the researchers have explored ways in which teachers and schools can move away from the damaging belief that learners can be categorised based on their perceived ability and that their position within ability grouping remains static (Drummond and Hart with Swann, 2013). Instead they advocate a school-wide community of learners, with an emphasis placed on supporting staff to develop children's individual learning needs to allow them to flourish (Drummond and Hart with Swann, 2013). Goodley (2011) similarly highlights the possibility of change in school culture by drawing on Apple's 'alternative social model of education' (1982: 173). Here an emphasis is placed on acceptance, tolerance and creativity rather than raising the performance of individuals (Booth in Clough and Corbett, 2000, as cited in Goodley, 2011). This position can be summarised with a quote from Stiker: '... difference is not an exception ... but something that happens in the natural course of things' (1997: 12). We need to recognise this as being something to be celebrated within our learning environments. No child is the same, and by suggesting all children should conform to the idea that there is a normal learner, we are denying children the opportunity to really thrive.

QUESTIONS FOR REFLECTION

1. Draw an image to represent your understanding of the key differences between the medical and social models of disability and the impact these have on the educational experiences of disabled children.

2. Think about your own educational experiences. Was your school inclusive? If yes, how did your school achieve this? If no, what changes would you make to ensure your school was more inclusive?

3. You have been asked to plan a session to be used in an early years setting that focuses on celebrating human diversity – what would you need to include?

SUMMARY

This chapter has provided an overview of how the position of disabled children has evolved throughout history. By doing so it has been highlighted to the reader how SEN/D has been historically constructed. Unfortunately, there is evidence presented in this chapter which suggests that disabled children are still likely to encounter oppression throughout their childhood and beyond. Due to the continuous emphasis placed on normalising childhood (and anything outside of these very narrow realms being considered abnormal) this leads to disabled children being 'othered'. Disabled children remain on the outskirts, not only in terms of their educational experiences, but also as regards their wider social encounters. As it stands our education system appears to be failing many disabled children as they continue to be segregated and excluded for not conforming to our expectations. It has been demonstrated, however, that there is another way, and with a change in school culture and attitudes it would be possible to achieve a truly inclusive education system for all children.

End of chapter glossary

*   **Disability** is termed when an individual's needs are made 'special' as a result of how we conceptualise and organise social systems.
*   **Disabled child** is understood as a child who has an impairment, for example a visual impairment, and is disabled by how society responds to their difference.
*   **Medical model of disability** emphasises the identification of what is 'wrong' with an individual and focuses on finding ways to 'fix' them.
*   **Social model of disability** emphasises the identification of the social structures that create disability.

Further reading

McLaughlin, J., Coleman-Fountain, E. and Clavering, E. (2016) *Disabled Childhoods: Monitoring Differences and Emerging Identities*. Abingdon: Routledge.

Priestley, M. (2003) *Disability: A Life Course Approach*. Cambridge: Polity.

Tomlinson, S. (2012) *A Sociology of Special Education*. Abingdon: Routledge.

References

Apple, M. (1982) *Education and Power*. Boston, MA: Routledge and Kegan Paul.

Barnes, C. (1997) 'A Legacy of Oppression: A History of Disability Studies in Western Culture'. In L. Barton and M. Oliver (eds), *Disability Studies: Past, Present and Future*. Leeds: The Disability Press.

Boaler, J., Wiliam, D. and Brown, M. (2000) Students' experiences of ability grouping: disaffection, polarisation and the construction of failure, *British Educational Research Journal*, 26 (5): 631–648.

Bolt, D. (2012) 'Social Encounters, Cultural Representation and Critical Avoidance'. In N. Watson, A. Roulstone and C. Thomas (eds), *Routledge Handbook of Disability Studies*. Abingdon: Routledge.

Cameron, C. (2014) *Disability Studies: A Student's Guide*. London: Sage.

Cantwell, D.P. (1999) Attention Deficient Disorder: a review of the past 10 years, *Journal of American Child and Adolescent Psychiatry*, 35 (2): 978–987.

Caslin, M. (2014) 'Behaviour, Emotion and Social Attitudes: The Education of "challenging" pupils'. In D. Bolt (ed.), *Changing Social Attitudes Toward Disability: Perspectives from Historical, Cultural, and Educational Studies*. Abingdon: Routledge.

Coad, J. and Lewis, A. (2004) Engaging Children and Young People in Research: Literature Review for the National Evaluation of the Children's Fund. Birmingham: University of Birmingham.

Connors, C. and Stalker, K. (2007) Children's experiences of disability: pointers to a social model of childhood disability, *Disability and Society*, 22 (1): 19–33.

Coppock, V. (2002) 'Medicalising Children's Behaviour'. In B. Franklin (ed.), *The New Handbook of Children's Rights: Comparative Policy and Practice* (2nd edition). London: Routledge.

Davis, J. and Watson, N. (2002) 'Countering Stereotypes of Disability: Disabled Children and Resistance'. In M. Corker and T. Shakespeare (eds), *Disability/Postmodernity: Embodying Disability Theory*. London: Continuum.

Davis, L. (2013) *The Disability Studies Reader* (4th edition). London: Verso.

Department for Education (DfE) (2016) *Special Educational Needs in England: January 2016*. London: Department of Education. Available at www.gov.uk/government/statistics/special-educational-needs-in-england-january-2016 (last accessed 15 August 2016).

Department for Education and Department of Health (DfE and DoH) (2015) *Special Educational Needs and Disability Code of Practice: 0 to 25 Years*. (Statutory guidance for organisations which work with and support children and young people who have special educational needs or disabilities.) London: Dfe/DoH. Available at www.gov.uk/government/uploads/system/uploads/attachment_data/file/398815/SEND_Code_of_Practice_January_2015.pdf (last accessed 29 March 2017).

Drummond, M.J. and Hart, S. with Swann, M. (2013) An alternative approach to school development: the children are the evidence, *FORUM for Promoting 3–19 Comprehensive Education*, 55 (1): 121–132.

Equality and Human Rights Commission (2015) *Is Britain Fairer? The State of Equality and Human Rights 2015*. London: Equality and Human Rights Commission. Available at www.equalityhumanrights.com/en/britain-fairer (accessed 29 March 2017).

Garland, R. (1995) *The Eye of the Beholder: Deformity and Disability in the Graeco-Roman World*. London: Duckworth.

Garland-Thomson, R. (1997) *Extraordinary Bodies: Figuring Physical Disability in American Literature and Culture*. New York: Columbia University Press.

Goodley, D. (2011) *Disability Studies: An Interdisciplinary Approach*. London: Sage.

Hill, M. and Tisdall, S. (1997) *Children and Society*. Longman: London.

Hodkinson, A. (2016) *Key Issues in Special Educational Needs and Inclusion* (2nd edition). London: Sage.

McLaughlin, J., Coleman-Fountain, E. and Clavering, E. (2016) *Disabled Childhoods: Monitoring Differences and Emerging Identities*. Abingdon: Routledge.

Miller, T. and Leger, M.C. (2003) A very childish moral panic: Ritalin, *Journal of Medical Humanities*, 24 (1): 9–33.

O'Connor, M., Hodkinson, A., Burton, D. and Torstensson, G. (2011) Pupil voice: listening to and hearing the educational experiences of young people with behavioural, emotional and social difficulties (BESD), *Emotional and Behavioural Difficulties*, 16: 289–302.

Oliver, M. (1990) *The Politics of Disablement*. London: Macmillan.

Penketh, C. (2014) Invention and repair: disability and education after the UK Coalition Government, *Disability and Society*, 29: 1486–1490.

Penketh, C. and Waite, L. (2015) 'Lessons in Critical Avoidance'. In D. Bolt and C. Penketh (eds), *Disability, Avoidance and the Academy: Challenging Resistance*. Abingdon: Routledge.

Priestley, M. (2003) *Disability: A Life Course Approach*. Cambridge: Polity.

Smith, M. (2012) *Hyperactive: The Controversial History of ADHD*. London: Reaktion.

Stiker, H.J. (1997) *A History of Disability*. Ann Arbor: University of Michigan Press.

Stanley, T. (2016) Down's Syndrome people risk 'extinction' at the hands of science, fear and ignorance, *Telegraph* (online), 18 January. Available at www.telegraph.co.uk/news/2016/03/22/downs-syndrome-people-risk-extinction-at-the-hands-of-science-fe/ (last accessed 29 March 2017).

Terzi, L. (2005) Beyond the dilemma of difference: the capability approach to disability and special educational needs, *Journal of Philosophy of Education*, 39 (3): 443–459.

Thomas, G. and Loxley, A. (2007) *Deconstructing Special Education and Constructing Inclusion* (2nd edition). Maidenhead: McGraw-Hill/Open University Press.

Timimi, S. (2009) A Straight Talking Introduction to Children's Mental Health Problems. Herefordshire: PCCS Books Ltd.

Tomlinson, S. (2012) *A Sociology of Special Education*. Abingdon: Routledge.

United Nations General Assembly (1989) *Convention on the Rights of the Child*, UN General Assembly, Document A/RES/44/25 [online]. Available at www.hrweb.org/legal/child.html (last accessed 29 March 2017).

Union of the Physically Impaired Against Segregation (UPIAS) (1976) *Fundamental Principals of Disability*. London: UPIAS.

5

THE REGULATED CHILD

CAROL AUBREY, CAROLYN BLACKBURN, CHARLOTTE JONES AND ROSEMARIE LOWE

CHAPTER OBJECTIVES

- To acknowledge that the concept of participation, as a right for children, is open to different interpretations and applications.

- To explore the principle that children have rights to participate in decision-making processes that may be relevant in their lives and to influence decisions taken in their regard within the family, the school or the community.

- To consider the view that participation may operate at different levels from macro-level statutory rights enshrined in policy, through meso-level local authority (LA) enactment of rights policy, to micro-level exercise of rights by individual children.

- To acknowledge that, in practice, the right to participation tends to be granted by the adults who have the responsibility to create enabling conditions intended to empower children.

- To consider the notion that children's rights remains an ideological position, and hence a contested and thus political area.

This chapter explores the concept of participation as a right for children. Given that child participation has various definitions and is applied to a variety of attitudes, values and behaviours, it will adopt a case-study approach. Firstly, it will draw upon an LA-funded project that investigated the participation of vulnerable children and young people (CYP) in the integrated frontline service provision they received. Secondly, it will examine core principles underpinning the *United Nations Convention on the Rights of the Child* (1989: Article 12), in order to examine statutory views of participation rights. By these means, the chapter will seek to investigate CYPs' exercise of participation rights as well as attempt to identify factors that might influence the exercise of participation. In so doing, the chapter will consider whether or not the statutory view provides the conditions for exercised rights.

The broader international context of children's participation in public service decision making

In order to consider the broader context of participation of CYP in public service decision making concerning their lives a search of literature for the period since 2004 was undertaken. The first, and most significant, finding focused on child participation in practice, set in the context of national and international policy. Studies were mainly empirical in nature, although they included conceptual analyses and meta-analyses of child participation research. A second finding involved literature that focused on critical analyses of the concept of child participation. Finally, and to a lesser extent, the literature focused on methodology, design or methods constructed to elicit children's voices. The studies highlighted below are illustrative of the broad range considered.

Child participation in practice

Reported practice in this group varied from country to country, from agency to agency, taking account of the age and competence of the CYP concerned. Social work and child protection were prominent topics (though the CAF process excludes CYP who might be suffering, or at risk of suffering harm that follows safeguarding procedures). Dominant here were the same concerns about confidentiality and information sharing expressed in the study by Newvell (2004). Charron (2011), for example, explored participation and decision making, intervention planning, and relationships with professionals in two Canadian provinces, with 16 young people aged between 14 and 17 years-old who were largely satisfied with their involvement. By contrast, Seim and Slettebø (2010) reported that Norwegian youth had hardly any experience of individual participation in decision making regarding child protection and regarded caseworkers as distant. Vis and Strandbu (2011) argued that child participation in protection proceedings had been difficult to achieve, but questioned the long-term effects of successful participation and potential side-effects, for which evidence was absent. Using examples from Australia, New Zealand and Nordic countries, Young et al. (2012) argued that protection of children in health and social work was bounded by risk factors, and hence investigative rather than preventative. Whilst participation of children in principle was acknowledged as a human right, in practice it was shown that it could unsettle well-being. Bell and Wilson (2006), investigating the views of 20 English children aged 6 to 16 years-old included in family group conferences, argued that whilst such conferences had a role they did not necessarily lead to empowering practice for all children and families. By contrast, Sanders and Mace (2006) reported a total lack of children's direct input into Welsh service planning for protection, with conferences being regarded as a barrier. Theobald, Danby and Ailwood (2011) reviewed the field of child participation in the Australian early education context, identifying a gap between policy supporting children's participation in decision making that affected them and actual everyday participation in classroom practice. Meanwhile, Coyne from the Irish perspective and Harder from the Swedish point of view suggested that children's participation in decision making in the healthcare field was complex because parents and professionals tended to act in children's 'best interests' and thus protectively. Coyne and Harder (2011) concluded that children preferred to be protected in some situations and take part in decision making in others. Their argument was for adoption of a situational perspective with account to be taken of children's rights, competence and preference.

Critical analysis of child participation

The section above reveals how balancing protection and participation may be hard to achieve in practice. Pölkki et al. (2012) stressed that in Finland children in care had a legal right to be consulted before decisions influencing their lives were made, in line with the *United Nations Convention on the Rights of the Child* (UNCRC) (1989). Interviewing CYP aged 7 to 17 years-old in family foster care, they found that whilst participation was very significant to them, they did not always want to be active participants, for example in meetings. Significantly, however, they felt that they were better listened to after placement than in the decision-making stages. Many serious obstacles to participatory work emerged. It was thought that on the one hand, loyalty to parents might prevent children from expressing their opinion, and on the other, that social workers might lack the skills, work practices and experience through which children's experiences, views and desires could be best represented. From the English perspective, Lewis (2010) interrogated the concept of 'child voice' and the purposes of engagement with children. Her recommendations to researchers in the field emphasised recognising, noting, responding to, interpreting and reporting silence from children. In the broader context of European researchers, Spyrou (2011) problematised what he described as a preoccupation with children's voice in child-centred research. Like Lewis, he called for more reflection and reflexivity in representation of children's voice, to take better account of the power imbalance that shaped voice and the contexts within which it was produced and received. Claims for authenticity needed to acknowledge the complex, multi-faceted and idiosyncratic nature of children's voice.

Matters of methodology

The critical papers above led to a consideration of a third group of methodology papers. Daly (2009), from the Australian perspective, noted that CYP were often the subjects of research, but not usually co-designers of research projects, questions or tools that are used to research their perspectives. He reported a small study of 14 CYP who had been in out-of-home care, from whom views on what makes a 'good' carer were sought. CYP as stakeholders in the foster-care system engaged creatively in devising individual and group activities and conversational contexts. By such means, it was argued, it should be possible to ensure that CYPs' views were of benefit to other CYP, practitioners and policy makers in the field. Other studies have examined methods used and activities devised to elicit accounts of the involvement of CYP in decision-making processes. Leeson (2007) used narratives, games and other activities to explore the thoughts and feelings of four young people whilst in the care of the LA. Participants considered how the care system might be constructed differently to facilitate their voice and the voice of much younger children. She concluded that the debate was one of adult ability and preparedness to involve CYP in decisions concerning their lives, rather than one of CYPs' capacity to participate effectively. Aubrey and Dahl (2006) explored views on service providers of 21 vulnerable English children of 11 years and younger, identified by the LA as 'at-risk', using a variety of decision charts, concrete rating scales and dictating a postcard message to a key worker that identified one good thing about current practice and one change that might be made. They questioned, however, whether CYPs' involvement served to increase a sense of autonomy or merely extended the extent to which they were controlled. Porter et al. (2008) set out to develop user-friendly data collection tools for disabled children of 5, 9 and 13 years-old with a range of communication needs accessed in a group, in pairs or individually. Online and hard-copy questionnaires allowed rating of school experiences using symbols of smiley and glum faces. It was acknowledged that flexible tools, embedded in meaningful activities, with some personalisation, were needed in order to promote self-reflection as well as a positive ethos.

This section has unearthed a number of tensions between CYPs' rights, competence and preference on the one hand, and professional concerns about balancing protection and participation of CYP on the other. Loyalty to family may lead to CYPs' reluctance to engage. Silence may be valid in certain circumstances. Professional expectations of CYPs' participation can take too little account of the power imbalance. As Leeson (2007) pointed out, the issue may be one of professional capacity, sensitivity and preparedness to involve CYP in decisions about their lives rather than one of CYPs' ability to participate. Overall, the discussion reveals the way in which micro-level, individual CYPs' views are mediated through a level of situated face-to-face interactions with professionals, in a broader social-setting or organisational level that carries rules, positions and practices reflecting a wider macro-level of resource allocation, underpinned by political and financial considerations that legitimate power and control.

Macro-level UK policy context for children's services

UK child and family policy, legislation and guidance have increasingly emphasised inter-agency co-operation and multi-agency teams as a significant feature of effective practice. A major impetus came from a commitment to children's services 'working together', in particular, in the interests of child protection. Within the legal framework of the Children Act (DfES, 2004) responsibility for most children's services was brought together under a Minister for Children, and at the LA level Directors for Children's Services were made responsible for planning and delivering integrated services through Children's Trusts. The guidance for Directors of Children's Services states:

The DCS should have regard to the General Principles of the United Nations Convention on the Rights of the Child (UNCRC) and ensure that children and young people are involved in the development and delivery of local services. (DfE, 2013: 5)

A framework of services 'supports' vulnerable children within a Common Assessment Framework (CAF), led by multi-agency teams with systems of information sharing and co-ordinated by a lead professional (LP). The CAF was designed to help practitioners assess CYPs' additional needs at an early stage and work with CYP and their families, along with other professionals and agencies, to meet these needs. The decision by professionals to undertake such an assessment should be taken in consultation with CYP and the family and comprises three stages: preparation for and gaining informed consent; carrying out the assessment; and identifying and intervening, where necessary, to address unmet needs or achieve better outcomes. As promotion of the participation of CYP has been central to the CAF process, staff in the LA should be keen to seek CYPs' views on services received.

Meso-level LA enactment of children's participation in decision making

A number of evaluations of the CAF have been carried out with the voices of CYP notably missing (e.g. Brandon et al., 2006; Easton et al., 2011). Holmes et al. (2012) interviewed 29 parents or carers in the context of an online survey of 237 professionals and undertook focus groups and interviews with CAF team members. The majority were positive about the process and regarded the LP highly. About one-half had attended a team-around-the-child (TAC) meeting and emphasised the need to be listened to appropriately. There was some concern that judgements made about parenting skills might be passed on to Social Services.

A study that did focus on the views of CYP and parents about the CAF was carried out by Newvell (2004). This involved 52 CYP between the ages of 11 and 19 years-old. It covered confidentiality, information sharing and consent, user involvement and the expectations of professionals completing the CAF. In general CYP were supportive of CAF, with reservations expressed about the process and the behaviour of professionals. They stressed that being recognised as an individual was important and not being treated the same as everyone else. They were concerned to maintain some sense of control over the process, its pace and outcomes, and in particular who would be told. Issues of consent and confidentiality were complex but it was found that clarity was needed.

Therefore, despite a policy emphasis that 'the safety and the educational, social and emotional needs of children and young people are central' (DfE, 2013: 4), the research evidence from children's perspectives is not abundant.

Micro-level investigation of case study CYPs' participation

The next section of the chapter will detail a case study project that was commissioned by an LA that recognised a significant need to explore their CAF procedure from the perspectives of CYP. It took place within the wider context of a pledge that 'we will ask children, young people and families about what works and what doesn't', with the intention being to contribute to service development. A participatory approach was adopted to facilitate CYPs' discussion of their views about CAF. 'Participation' covers a wide variety of practices but its core process is to enable participants to share their perceptions of an identified problem area, reach a common understanding and suggest a potential solution (Laws et al., 2013). It is particularly suited for groups who may not typically feel empowered to voice opinions or take action. It is intended to be facilitative and has a commitment to share power and initiative with others. A balance inevitably has to be achieved between users, in this case CYP and the CAF agenda of the LA concerned. A range of methods was adapted to this approach.

A sample of CYP were selected from the LA's database by its Integrated Working Team, based on a breakdown of CAF data by age and nature of vulnerability, and included children with special educational needs (SEN). The sample included inner-city, suburban and semi-rural schools on the edge of the LA, with a diverse mix of pupils. A total of 39 CYP across the age range, from pre- to post-school, took part in the project. For illustrative purposes, this chapter will focus in more depth on 15 primary-aged children (5 to 11 years-old) and eight of secondary age (12 to 16 years-old). Of the primary-aged children eight had learning difficulties, six of these had English as an additional language (EAL), six had social-emotional and behavioural difficulties, and one had health-related difficulties. All eight of those of secondary age had social-emotional and behavioural difficulties, in two cases poor attendance was involved, and for another two low self-esteem was highlighted. A further five preschoolers had been identified, but discussion with the family support worker established that whilst CAF procedures were initiated when a child reached two years, the focus of intervention was the family, parent or caregiver, not the young child.

For all age groups, a menu of activities was created from which participants selected. The CAF conversation was loosely structured around the CAF process: 'before the CAF', 'at the start of CAF', 'during CAF', 'at the end of CAF', and 'after CAF, some reflections', though in practice most had not completed the process. The secondary-aged CYP selected from the following:

- A 'time-line for change' activity to map the journey through the CAF stages on a large poster, using text, cartoons, drawings or stickers to describe and decorate key points along the way, positive and negative experiences and progress made.
- An 'evaluation cake' with segments corresponding to the same points in the CAF process to indicate aspects liked least and most, together with a star rating for each and an explanation.
- Creation of an oral self-presentation with a partner, using a flip camera and a laminated question card as prompts for the same CAF stages.

The primary-aged children selected from the following:

- An oral, modified version of the CAF process was presented after first checking familiarity with the terminology and offering a brief, simplified account of the process. Questions covered the same stages – did you know what was happening and why you were having this (CAF); did you go to the meetings; how did you feel about this; did people listen to you; could you ask questions; who was the main person who helped you make things better; do you think that it is better now at home/school; can you say how; is there anything else that would help to make things better? Where appropriate, children were provided with a flowerpot and beans and invited to rate their CAF experience in terms of its quality (no beans, or one to three beans). The family-support worker was on hand to prompt, remind or link to shared experience.
- For one 5 year-old with complex difficulties, photographs of significant adults, school and a centre that he attended were used for visual elicitation. He was able to respond to simple questions about places, persons and related activities and rate them in terms of star stickers, whilst explaining to a friendly puppet what he needed to know in order to have a good time at the venue concerned.

Common themes emerged across the age range, others were characteristic of particular age groups. All students had difficulty in understanding key CAF terminology and were unclear about: the process; its initiation; people and events within the process; and when and how closure came about. An amount of congruence was observed across the groups in the nature of the presenting problem, relating to home, family and interpersonal relationships, but affecting progress and adjustment in school too.

Understanding, awareness and involvement in the CAF processes increased with age, with secondary-aged CYP willing to acknowledge ownership of the presenting problem and actively engage in its modification. Whilst none of the secondary-aged CYP remembered being consulted about initiation of the CAF, all had attended some CAF meetings. Although they were not positive about this experience nor did they feel listened to, all were of the view that life at school and home had improved. Of the 15 primary-aged children, two reported attending meetings and shared the same unfavourable view of this experience. Nine showed no understanding of the CAF processes, whilst four, when prompted by the family-support worker, showed some awareness of their family's involvement, and three described implementation of home-based behaviour-management programmes (for instance, a behaviour chart with rules, a 'naughty step' for time-out and a star chart for good behaviour).

Secondary-aged CYP selected from the menu of options to represent their CAF experience. Two chose to video-interview one another; another group of three to represent the journey through CAF in cartoon form with speech bubbles. Two selected the 'cake' to depict the stages of the CAF process, whilst another one mapped out and reflected on her CAF journey with its personal, social and academic benefits.

For primary-aged children a particular challenge was to establish a form of words that was mutually comprehensible. Where links could be established to wider home and school issues, it was possible to ask them to rate their experiences with dried beans. For the youngest child of 5 years-old, extensive preparation involved securing photographs of significant adults and placement settings, the use of favourite cartoon characters, a puppet, stickers, stamps and labels, to enable him to identify familiar and trusted adults and rate educational programmes and settings.

CASE STUDY 5.1   EXPLORING THE VOICES OF CASE STUDY CYP

As noted above, secondary-aged students and one older primary-aged student were participating in the CAF process, and maintained responsibility for self-monitoring of behaviour and hence the success of the programme concerned. Their experience of CAF meetings had not however been altogether positive.

Case study CYPs recalled their experience at the start of the process

'I was told I was going to be on a CAF and I was unsure.'

'I was shy and I never knew what was going on.'

'I was without a school placement for a long time.'

'Once CAF was explained, I calmed down. I was about to be kicked out of school. When I heard about CAF, I was worried ... thought something bad was about to happen.'

'I didn't know why they were doing it ... why I was having it.'

'Never knew what was going on. Then the point came, so I was getting there.'

'I was told – don't worry, I'm going to put you in CAF.'

'Getting started was unusual at first. CAF was explained and I was nervous but I got allowed back into school. My key worker organised this CAF to see if I could get help.'

'I thought I would sit down, play games ... go for a walk whilst you are talking.'

Reflections on CAF meetings were varied

'I was glad meetings were happening so I could get a better chance of closing the CAF.'

'I never knew who was in the meeting.'

'So CAF can help you in many ways, like behaviour and attitude.'

'It gives me targets and I've achieved most of them.'

'Nothing had happened like this before. Everyone was looking at me. I was scared and nervous.'

In terms of achievements, CYPs' recollections were more positive

'They did what they said they would do because it was planned well. It really helped me. There was a big difference.'

'There were a lot of meetings. Things were getting better.'

'People sorted out my problems. I felt fine. It was great, just great.'

'Nice people ... I'm glad someone helped me.'

'Yes, they listened. Everyone helped me ... I worked things out myself ... what to do.'

'Towards the end, students could appreciate the benefits.'

'I am happy about CAF. I behave better. CAF has helped me to improve my behaviour.'

'CAF changed me ... if it wasn't for CAF I wouldn't be sitting in this chair now. I would be out of school with no education. I still feel like I'm trapped at break and lunch ... no freedom ... time to chill out with friends. But school is about learning so I'm doing my best to get my General Certificate of Secondary Education'.

'Finally, there were no more meetings and things got much better.'

Judging by CYPs' responses, they did not have CAF terms and processes explained in an age-appropriate manner and in advance. One primary-aged child, when asked what CAF meant, replied 'You go there and, like, have a drink and that ... ' In other words, he confused CAF with a café. There was little evidence of modifications being made to meetings of professionals to include and increase the accessibility to participation of CYP. These CYP did not appear to be able to exercise their right to express their views in all matters affecting them or to have due weight given to these in accordance with their age and maturity (UN, 1989). Working flexibly did help them to depict their CAF journeys, in pictures and text, with younger children assisted by a scribe. Central to this was the need to listen carefully. This empowered them and increased their confidence, self-esteem and well-being.

These findings question the current definitions, terms and professional meanings provided for vulnerable CYP. They also question the adequacy of CAF procedures in terms of the rights of vulnerable CYP. In the context of CAF, they have a right to be allowed to make an active contribution to their home and school lives and to improve the professional services they receive. The participatory approach used served to address some of the power imbalance between the researchers and CYP, compounded where the adult is a professional who is able to make powerful decisions about home and school.

Involving CYP more fully in CAF processes would ensure that decisions made remained grounded in their lived experiences. Allowing them to help identify appropriate methodologies for gathering views also ensured that the tools constructed were relevant. Flexibility allowed not only for variety in response but also for the variation in social context so that CYP worked as individuals, pairs or trios. By such means they shared insights and perspectives that were accessible to one another. Incorporating CYPs' perspectives acknowledges that child, home and family, school and professionals, provide complementary perspectives to ensure that the best decisions about their lives are made.

More fundamentally, the project findings suggest that the universal and absolute right for the child in regard to participation, in practice, is tempered by age and maturity. Whilst all children must be treated with equal respect, irrespective of their age and competency, they must understand the ground rules and power relations established at the beginning. Participation must be voluntary and children must be allowed to leave at any time. This suggests that adults must grant and indeed facilitate participation and take active steps to enable and empower children.

Participation as a statutory right?

From the statutory rights perspective, child participation and hence power relations between adults and children are legally regulated. In this respect, the UNCRC (UN, 1989) stands as a landmark and several provisions reflect children's right to participate as a guiding principle and a challenge. The Convention has 54 articles that cover all aspects of a child's life and set out rights that all children everywhere are entitled to, regardless of their ethnicity, gender, religion, language or abilities. It also indicates how adults and governments must work together to make sure all children can benefit from all of their rights. Children's rights are thereby legally bound in respect of three *Ps*: *Provision* (of food, health care and education); *Protection* (from child labour or abuse); and *Participation* (for example, in expressing views, exercising choice and making decisions).

CASE STUDY 5.2   EXPLORING INTERNATIONAL PARTICIPATION POLICY

Article 12 of the UNCRC (Respect for the views of the child) states that children have the right to participate in decision-making processes that may be relevant in their lives and to influence decisions taken in their regard, within the family, the school or the community.

The principle affirms that children do have a right to express their views in all matters affecting them, and requires those hearing them to give due weight to these according to age and maturity. As the UNICEF fact sheet acknowledges:

It recognizes the potential of children to enrich decision-making processes, to share perspectives and to participate as citizens and actors of change. The practical meaning of children's right to participation must be considered in each and every matter concerning children. (2014:1)

The fact sheet goes on to emphasise that participation is an underlying value that guides the way rights are ensured and respected, and a criterion by which to assess progress in implementation in relation to the children's views being heard and taken into account. Through a process of dialogue and exchange, adults give direction and guidance so that children's views may influence decisions, and in turn they may gain understanding of the decision-making process.

This chapter has considered different perspectives on the right to participate, drawn attention to various levels of participation, and in particular has focused on statutory and exercised rights. In so doing it has uncovered some of the factors that influence participation. It has pointed to the real challenge professionals face in establishing partnerships with children, and specifically to the dimension of participation as a 'granted' right.

QUESTIONS FOR REFLECTION

1. Do you think that the case study CYP were empowered by the CAF or merely regulated?

2. Should CYPs' participation in CAF processes be restricted by age, maturity or presumed understanding?

3. In practice, how willing are adults to listen to children's points of view and take action on the basis of these?

4. What if children do not wish to participate?

5. What sort of training might be required by professionals in order to ensure that the methods they use to elicit the views, intentions and opinions of young children are appropriate?

SUMMARY

Some CYP are participating in decision making concerning their lives, but practice is uneven. Participation is influenced by national policy, the agency involved, and the age and competence of the CYP concerned. Research has found that participation is more common in older CYP of 12 years-old and over. Also, giving voice to CYP with SEN, disabilities and EAL poses particular challenges.

It has been found that relevant professional practice may not yet be embedded or incorporated at higher strategic levels. Additionally, children do not always want to be consulted or attend meetings as the experience is not necessarily rewarding, empowering or regarded as a positive force in their lives. However, it can be concluded that a lack of involvement can increase powerlessness, contribute to a lack of confidence and lower self-esteem. Thus satisfaction from involvement in decision making varies, as does the degree of involvement experienced.

End of chapter glossary

- **Exercised rights** relate to children's active involvement in the real contexts of home or school.
- **Granted rights** are what are applied in practice and concern adult–child relationships in a particular society.
- **Participation** as a concept and as a right for children is complex and has different meanings for different people.
- **Statutory rights** are achieved through national, European or international legislation.

Further reading

Davey, C., Burke, T. and Shaw, C. (2010) *Children's Participation in Decision-Making: A Children's Views Report*. London: Participation Works. Available at www.childrens commissioner.gov.uk/sites/default/files/publications/Childrens_participation_in_decision-making_-_A_childrens_views_report.pdf (last accessed 20 October 2016).

Hudson, K. (2012) Evidence Briefing: Participation of children and young people in policy development and implementation, Conversations Project Report, 4. Available at www.gov.scot/Publications/2012/06/1592/4 (last accessed 20 October 2016).

UN Children's Fund (UNICEF) (2014) *Fact Sheet: The Right to Participation*. Available at www.unicef.org/crc/files/Right-to-Participation.pdf (last accessed 20 October 2016).

References

Aubrey, C. and Dahl, S. (2006) Children's voices: the views of vulnerable children on their service providers and the relevance of services they receive, *British Journal of Social Work*, 36 (1): 21–39.

Bell, M. and Wilson, K. (2006) Children's views of family group conferences, *British Journal of Social Work*, 36 (4): 671–681.

Brandon, M., Howe, A., Dagley, V., Salter, C., Warren, C. and Black, J. (2006) *Evaluating the CAF: Research Report RR740*. London: Department for Education and Skills/ University of East Anglia.

Charron, L. (2011) *How Youth Involved in Child Protection Services Are Included in Intervention Planning and Decision-Making*. Montreal, Canada: McGill University.

Coyne, I. and Harder, M. (2011) Children's participation in decision-making, *Journal of Child Health Care*, 15 (14): 312–319.

Daly, W. (2009) Adding their flavour to the mix: involving children and young people in care in research design, *Australian Social Work*, 62 (4): 460–475.

Department for Education (DfE) (2013) *Statutory Guidance on the Roles and Responsibilities of the Director of Children's Services and the Lead Member for Children's Services*. London: DfE.

Department for Education and Skills (DfES) (2004) *Children Act*. London: DfES.

Easton, C., Gee, G., Durbin, B. and Teeman, D. (2011) *Early Intervention, using the CAF Process, and its Cost-Effectiveness: Findings from LARC3*. Slough: NFER.

Holmes, L., McDermid, S., Padley, M. and Soper, J. (2012) *Exploration of the Costs and Impact of the CAF*. London: Department for Education.

Laws, S., Harper, C., Jones, N. and Marcus, R. (2013) *Research for Development: A Practical Guide* (2nd edition). London: Sage.

Leeson, C. (2007) My life in care: experiences of non-participation in decision-making processes, *Child and Family Social Work*, 12 (3): 268–277.

Lewis, A. (2010) Silence in the context of 'child voice', *Children and Society*, 24 (1): 14–23.

Newvell, J. (2004) *National Children's Bureau: Report on the Common Assessment Framework – Consultation with Children, Young People and Parents*. London: National Children's Bureau.

Pölkki, P., Vornanen, R., Pursianen, M. and Riikonen, M. (2012) Children's participation in child-protection processes as experienced by foster children and social workers, *Child and Youth Services Review*, 32 (7): 107–125.

Porter, J., Daniels, H., Georgeson, J., Hacker, J., Gallop, V., Feiler, A., Tarleton, B. and Watson, D. (2008) *Disability Data Collection for Children's Services: Report RR062*. London: Department for Children, Families and Schools.

Sanders, R. and Mace, S. (2006) Agency policy and the participation of children and young people in the child protection process, *Child Abuse Review*, 15 (2): 26–36.

Seim, S. and Slettebø, T. (2010) Collective participation in child protection services: partnership or tokenism?, *European Journal of Social Work*, 10 (4): 497–512.

Spyrou, S. (2011) The limits of children's voice: from authenticity to critical, reflexive representation, *Childhood*, 18 (2): 151–165.

Theobald, M., Danby, S. and Ailwood, J. (2011) Child participation in the early years: challenges for education, *Australasian Journal of Early Childhood*, 36 (3): 89–26.

United Nations (UN) (1989) *UN Convention on the Rights of the Child*. Geneva: UN.

UN Children's Fund (UNICEF) (2014) *Fact Sheet: The Right to Participation*. Available at www.unicef.org/crc/files/Right-to-Participation.pdf (last accessed 28 March 2017).

Vis, S.A. and Strandbu, A. (2011) Participation and health – a research review of child participation in planning and decision-making, *Child and Family Social Work*, 16 (3): 325–335.

Young, S., McKenzie, M., Schjedlderup, L. and Omre, C. (2012) The rights of the child enabling community development to contribute to a valid social work practice with children at risk, *European Journal of Social Work*, 15 (2): 169–184.

6

THE STRESSED CHILD

NINA SAJANIEMI

CHAPTER OBJECTIVES

- To reveal the importance of the biological roots of behaviour.
- To underline the relevance of stress response regulation on learning for children.
- To emphasise the preventive role of early education.
- To introduce an integrative framework to learning and development.

It is a well-known but still underrated fact that the basis for future well-being and lifelong learning is built during early childhood, both at home and in nurseries, kindergartens and preschools (Erel et al., 2000; Campbell et al., 2001). Brain development is certainly most plastic during the early years. However, brain plasticity is a double-edged sword – the interaction between individual characteristics, environment and adult support moulds the plasticity towards resilience or maladaptive forms of behaviour and learning (Siegel, 2012). The surrounding environment can, undoubtedly, impact on the way the brain develops as well as how that brain is transformed into a unique human mind. It should be emphasised that children have an absolute need for adult support and adults have responsibility in cultivating or abolishing the enormous brain potential that every child has. Childhood education and care settings have a significant opportunity, therefore, for boosting holistic well-being and in opening pathways for lifelong learning.

Learning takes place in the brain. When something is learned or when experiences are printed in the memory, the brain forms new nerve connections and prunes away unnecessary or distracting ones. This leads, over time, to the establishment of new abilities and the enhancement of older ones. Brains are continuously developing and changing. They are also considerably shaped by doing and by the experiences of daily life (Siegel, 2012). At a microcellular level, the infinitely complex network of nerve cells that make up the constituent parts of the brain actually change in response to certain experiences and stimuli (Siegel, 2010). New levels of information processing and integration come online and hence   every   moment matters. The brain is literally use-dependent and only frequently activated synaptic connections between nerve cells are established long term. Pruning of non-activated connections diminishes alternatives and streamlines connections. Therefore the established nerve connections are the basis of all habits, routines, memories and learned content. Within this context it should be understood that a young child's brain is fragile. As it is exposed to environmental stimuli it is fundamentally important to protect the brain from the overloading of information and the overtaxing of experience. The adult's responsibility is to interact with children in a way that helps them regulate their stress responses, develop resilience, and extinguish maladaptive forms of behaviour (Nelson et al., 2014).

CASE STUDY 6.1   EXPLORING THE ECONOMIC FACTOR

Early Childhood Education and Care (ECEC) seeks to support children's right to be respected, valued, seen, heard and supported. Economists have stated for a long time that investment in ECEC will significantly pay off in the future in economic terms (Campbell et al., 2014). It is known that quality ECEC is effective in increasing equality, boosting learning, narrowing social class differences, and decreasing social exclusion (Syrjämäki et al., 2016). Quality ECEC has evident positive and long-lasting effects on well-being, heath-related behaviour, peer relationships and school achievement (Sylva et al., 2010). However, low-quality early education might have jeopardising effects on children's development. ECEC centres should not, therefore, be child storage facilities for when parents need someone else to take care of their children. In extreme cases, low-quality ECEC can cause functional brain damage through unregulated stress responses. Insensitive adults and environmental overloads compromise children's fragile brain development through immature neurobiological stress-sensitive systems. Every adult is, whether they realise it or not, a sculptor of the child's brain. To be a good sculptor it is important to know the material you have in your hands. Therefore, it is essential to understand the basis of brain-body-behaviour functions and their dependence on social interactions.

The stressful world challenges education

Human brains have been changing, adapting and developing in response to outside stimuli for centuries. However, the speed of change in the outside environment, particularly in relation to the development of new technologies, has increased dramatically. This change will affect human brains and behaviour over the next hundred years in ways that mankind might never have imagined. Brains are under the influence of an ever-expanding world of new technology: multichannel television, video games, MP3 players, the internet, wireless social networks, Bluetooth links – the list is endless. The immense flow of information, rapidly spreading news about human catastrophes, continuous changes in working life, together with possible economic concerns, are stressful, exhausting and energy consuming. Diminishing energy causes brain fatigue and compromises the stress-sensitive neurobiological system, leading to stress-induced behavioural, emotional and cognitive dysfunctions and mental confusion, and exacerbates feelings of insecurity. If the underlying origins are not addressed, the condition will persist to the point that the individual is affected negatively in a whole range of aspects of their life.

Environmental overload, a lack of social support, poor parenting and low-quality education, all leading to childhood stress, are especially injurious during the childhood years when brain development is still fragile and the basis of future life management is established (Dougherty et al., 2013). Most children spend a large part of their waking hours in educational environments where there is an immense flow of information, diversity of social relationships and plurality of situations. These can burden the developing and still immature social and emotional functions of children. It is of utmost importance that these environments are supportive, creative and adequately challenging (Sajaniemi et al., 2012; Sajaniemi et al., 2011). In a changing world there is a need to reappraise educational goals. Instead of focusing on boosting academic skills, the emphasis should be on promoting social abilities, adaptability, resilience and stress response regulation – all of these are the basis for lifelong learning (Blair, 2010). In addition, focusing on morals, ethics and values in a modern, shattered and polarised society is more important than ever. Learning to master one's own reactions, emotions and behaviour in a variety of everyday activities is important to understand in relation to the social uniqueness of the human mind.

Advances in biology and neuroscience have evidenced how children's brain and cognitive development are shaped by their learning experiences and environment (Sajaniemi et al., 2015). The debate about nature versus nurture is no longer fruitful since it is known that nature – the DNA, RNA – is much more fluid and complex through epigenetic regulation than has ever been thought before (Meaney, 2010). Consequently, thinking, learning and acting affect the brain and its capacities. The latest findings in biology and cognitive science raise fundamental questions about education, such as the preconditions of learning, the role of stress response, emotion regulation in learning, and especially what can be done to improve learning, well-being and social justice.

About the brain

Brains have evolved as active information-gathering devices; they simultaneously act and make predictions about the consequences of their actions based on internal models. In the most fundamental sense, learning occurs when the observed consequences of actions are inconsistent with the predictions of the models and so require change. The learner has to accommodate their own actions to find a new way to reach their goals when something unexpected or unpredicted happens. The educational task is to sustain and make use of instinct capability rather than to suppress it. The brain is the only truly changing organ; it has billions of neurons and near-infinite possibilities for synaptic interconnections and networks.

The brain has more biological possibilities than will ever be used and it is culturally moulded through use or disuse (Siegel, 2012).

The brain processes information that is brought in via the senses. Senses of vision, hearing, taste, smell, and touch connect us to the physical world. Kinaesthetic sense relates to the movements of the body. The interoceptive input from the muscles, bones and the internal organs, together with a wide range of hormonal, immune, metabolic and cardiovascular signals, transmits information about the bodily state that directly impacts on the brain's functioning and preconditions of learning. Human beings are embedded in social interaction through social senses that shape the brain throughout their lifetime. The mirror neuron system makes emotional ties between people possible and is a prerequisite for empathy and compassion (Siegel, 2010).

In addition, human beings process risk information about the environment, especially in relation to other people, continuously and subconsciously. In all new situations the sensory organs immediately begin an observational process that evaluates whether it is safe to engage or not. This process is initiated by our sense organs, which then communicate rapidly with the brain and peripheral nervous system, which informs the rest of the body, directing the behaviour towards the next action required to keep us safe. This process of perception and evaluation has been named as neuroception (Porges, 2004). It describes how neural circuits distinguish whether situations or people are safe, dangerous or life threatening. The rapid response hardware and software integration takes place in the lower parts of our brain that work at a subconscious level. It is fundamentally important that learning environments are signalling safety rather than stress through high-quality and sensitive pedagogy. If their social and psychological safety is not guaranteed, children are hardwired to fight, flight or freeze. During this reactive state of mind, it is impossible to be responsive and it is also impossible to learn.

Brain architecture and skills are built in a bottom-up sequence. Neural circuits that process basic information are wired earlier than those that process complex information. Higher circuits are always built on lower ones and advanced skills are built on basic skills in all aspects of development. Adaptation at higher skill levels is more difficult if lower-level circuits are not wired properly due to overwhelming stress (Sajaniemi et al., 2015). The circuits at the brainstem level are active from the beginning of life and they remain active throughout life. The brainstem plays an important role in the regulation of cardiac and respiratory function. In addition, it regulates the central nervous system and is pivotal to maintaining consciousness and regulating the sleep cycle. The next level is the limbic system that surrounds the cerebral hemispheres and the brainstem. Limbic regions play an important role in mediating emotions, motivation and memory. It has a key role in the appraisal of meaning, social processing and stress response regulation. The slowly maturing upper brain structures toward the top of the brain, such as the cerebral cortex, mediate more complex information-processing functions such as perception, thinking and reasoning (Siegel, 2012).

This basic architecture in the brain is laid down during the early years. Interpersonal experiences continue to influence how brains function throughout life, but the major structures – especially those that are responsible for stress response regulation – are initially formed in the early years. During development higher-order functions are based on lower-order functions. This process is most flexible early in life, but as the maturing brain becomes more specialised to assume more complex functions, it is less capable of reorganising and adapting to new or unexpected challenges. Genes and early experiences, therefore, shape the way neurons connect to one another and form the specialised circuits that give rise to mental processes. Brain circuits stabilise with age, making them increasingly more difficult to alter. Early plasticity means that it is easier and more effective to influence young children's developing brain architecture than to rewire parts of its circuitry in the adult years. The window of opportunity for development remains open during childhood, but the cost of remediation increases with age (Johnson et al., 2015).

Hence the unified brain functions as an interconnected and integrated system of hierarchical subsystems. Emotional well-being, attachment and feelings of belonging provide a strong foundation for emerging cognitive abilities, and together they form the basis for the foundation of human development. The emotional and physical health, social competencies and cognitive-linguistic capacities that emerge in the early years are all important prerequisites for success in school and later in the workplace and community. High-quality early education is thus a powerful tool in shaping the brain towards resilience and future achievements in children from non-privileged socio-economic backgrounds. It is more efficient, both biologically and economically, to ensure supportive educational environments during the early years than to try to fix the shortcomings of low-quality environments later (Hermida et al., 2015).

Stress responses – the double edged sword

Scientists have shown that chronic, unceasing stress in childhood, caused by extreme poverty, repeated abuse, severe maternal depression, negligent care or other inappropriate demands, for example, can be detrimental to the developing brain. However, moderate, short-term physiological responses to changing environmental stimuli are important and a necessary aspect of healthy development. Regulated stress responses are positive and a necessary feature for learning and well-being, since accelerating the stress-reactive neurobiological system gives a push to all activities by preparing the body to function (Sajaniemi et al., 2015).

Two physiological parameters related to stress response regulation include autonomic arousal, associated with acute, short-term responses (from the Sympatho–Adrenal–Medullary (SAM) axis), and more chronic, longer-term responses (from the Hypothalamus–Pituitary–Adrenal (HPA) axis). Despite some overlap, these two axes represent different, although complementary, aspects of the response to stress, and may be indicators of balanced or unbalanced stress response regulation. Responses from both the SAM and HPA axes originate from the hypothalamus, where sensory inputs and serum-based feedback mechanisms monitor both the level of environmental demand and the internal state of the organism.

In response to alarming stimuli, the SAM axis acts very quickly via the Sympathetic Nervous System (SNS) branch of the Autonomic Nervous System. Effects of the SAM axis include rapidly increased sweating on the palms and feet and dilation of the pupils, as well as an increase in heart rate, blood flow and oxygen uptake in the lungs (Bright et al., 2014).

The HPA axis is also instigated from the hypothalamus, based upon external environmental and internal monitoring inputs. The HPA axis responds more slowly to stressors than the SAM axis and does so via hormones rather than nerves (Nater and Rohleder, 2009). A cascade of responses begins in the hypothalamus and moves to the pituitary gland and adrenal cortex, from where cortisol is released into the bloodstream. Cortisol has significant effects on brain activation, especially on hippocampal areas and the prefrontal cortex, which are both fundamental to learning and memory. As a consequence of small amounts of cortisol, the hippocampal areas make learning processes possible. When regulated, the increasing amounts of cortisol trigger a negative feedback loop that ceases the detrimental responses and helps to maintain an optimal internal state (Herman and Cullinan, 1997; Gunnar and Fisher, 2006).

The activation of the stress response regulation system prepares the body to protect the organism against an experienced threat. Perceived changes in environmental stimuli, loud noises, exclusion and neglect, for example, all linked to stress, are experienced as threats that trigger an immediate response to fight, flee or freeze. These responses are energy consuming and they prevent human beings from utilising the higher-order prefrontal function. Without learning to regulate these responses, it is difficult to be attentive, think, learn and take others into consideration. At a behavioural level, signs of overt stress reactivity are diverse, including defiance, resistance, aggressiveness, manipulation, anxiety and withdrawal, as examples (Dougherty et al., 2013; Bright et al., 2014; Doom and Gunnar, 2014; Hill-Soderlund et al., 2015).

Learning to master biological roots

One of the most fundamental abilities that a human needs for future life management is stress response regulation. It is an acquired ability that develops only in attuned social interactions. In the absence of the buffering protection of sensitive adults, chronically unregulated stress responses become built into the body by processes that subsequently jeopardise the architecture of the developing brain. Adaptive response strategies to environmental challenges and stress are socially regulated in humans. In response, the social engagement system is activated through the ventral component of the vagal nerve (VVC), which is the most important parasympathetic nerve. The VVC, with its mechanisms of signalling and communication, provides the initial response to the environment, and the vagal brake inhibits, at the level of the heart, the strong mobilisation responses of the sympathetic nervous system (Porges, 2007).

The social engagement system not only provides direct social contact with others, but also modulates the physiological state to support positive social behaviour by exerting an inhibitory effect on the sympathetic nervous system. Perceived threats often result in a neural dissolution from the more recently developed systems of positive social behaviour and social communication, to the more primitive fight, flight and avoidance systems. In challenging, stressful moments young children have difficulty in inhibiting their fight or flight responses, especially when responsive and engaged adults are not present. They have not yet learned to use the vagal brake on their own. The resulting reactive behaviour is far too often misinterpreted as a clinical symptom of a behavioural or emotional disorder, although a child is only reacting in a way that is biologically appropriate at that very moment, without the guidance of the still immature prefrontal regulative connections (Sajaniemi et al., 2015).

During reactive states of behaviour, instigated by stress, there are ruptures, therefore, in connections and a lack of prefrontal regulation. Children are then not responsive, cautious or thoughtful. They do not have the capacity to listen, reflect and obey. It has been shown that the worst thing to do in these moments, when a child exhibits a reactive state of behaviour, is to isolate them as a punishment. Isolation is biologically alarming and it does not help children to learn ways to navigate the situation with others (Repo and Sajaniemi, 2015). On the contrary, isolation strengthens the tendency to be reactive when something unexpected or uncomfortable is happening. The responsibility of the adults present is to help children to slow down when they recognise that children are exhibiting a reactive state that is out of their control. Emotional expressiveness plays a crucial role in calming children and repairing ruptures in the social connection. The vagus nerve innervates facial muscles and muscles in the larynx. In a state of vagal brake, the voice and facial expressions are signalling safety, thus boosting social engagement. When the social engagement system is activated in a child's brain-body system, they are able to calm and can then become ready to listen and understand. Professionals should, therefore, understand the power of voice and facial expressions and use these instruments consistently when working with children in this situation (Sajaniemi et al., 2015).

Zone of proximal development

Young children have much to learn. Educational settings are optimal environments for sharing joy, happiness and experiences with peers and professionals. They are settings to learn to be with others, to play, to create, to explore and to learn various cognitive skills. Simultaneously, they have to learn to tolerate everyday troubles and displeasure. Drifting towards the upper limits of their current capacities and confronting minor conflicts can load the stress sensitive system. Children are supposed to regulate their behaviour in all kinds of relationships, both with other children and with adults. They have to communicate their feelings, intentions and thoughts in various social contexts. Further, they are forced to adjust their needs to daily routines and learn the facts, rules and behavioural strategies of the socio-cultural environment they are living in. While these challenges may accelerate the development of social and cognitive skills, they may also tax the child's emotional resources and adaptive competencies, thereby activating the stress-sensitive physiological system (Sajaniemi et al., 2012).

Timed and adequate responses to children's expressions indicating physiological change enhance the capacity to approach, tolerate and incorporate new challenges. The regulation of stress responses is a prerequisite not only for optimal social development, but also for cognitive development (Hotulainen et al., 2014). If the professional does not understand the biological needs of children, the stress responses are unbalanced and the level of stress hormones might remain elevated for a prolonged amount of time. Unbalanced responses endanger optimal brain development, especially on prefrontal areas, causing attention deficit, learning difficulties and behavioural disturbances (Koss et al., 2016). Concerns about stress-related behavioural disorders are rising. It has been documented that up to 22% of preschool aged children may suffer from anxiety, depression, or aggressive or defiant behaviour. Generally, there are increasing developmental and public health concerns over both internalising and externalising disorders, and stress-sensitive or stress-induced problems for children. These, in turn, can be seen as a part of the early onset of social polarisation (McClelland et al., 2000; Petresco et al., 2004; Paulus et al., 2015).

CASE STUDY 6.2 EXPLORING THE IMPORTANCE OF EDUCATION QUALITY

Research at the University of Helsinki, together with a growing number of international studies, has revealed that children's stress response regulation is strongly associated with early education quality (Sajaniemi et al., 2013). Although the majority of children in the study undertaken indicate typical stress response regulation, there are stress-vulnerable children in every group (Sajaniemi et al., 2011). These children seem to be especially sensitised to contextual cues and emotional signals. The children with unbalanced stress response regulation in the studies have compromised abilities to play, to participate and to act in the zone of proximal development. It is essential to identify these children early on because they may be at risk of long-term, undesirable developmental outcomes (Suhonen et al., 2016). The research undertaken at the University of Helsinki has shown in preliminary tests that quality improvement and increasing pedagogical sensitivity tend to have positive effects on stress response regulation and future development.

Foundations for learning

It is essential to target foundational abilities during early education. Conscious learning, sustained attention, executive function, thinking, waiting and problem solving develop when stress responses are regulated, and when children can strive towards goals without withdrawal or without turning to instant, easy solutions. Therefore adults have to proactively help children to use their vagal brake through positive social engagement. In this situation children can learn to be active and relaxed simultaneously, without the compulsion to fight, flee or freeze. This balanced stress response regulation brings stress resilience. It is the physiological underpinning of the various inner capacities needed for flexible adaptation to the diversity of environmental challenges. Enhancing stress response regulation refers to the capability of controlling one's arousal, attention, emotions and executive functions, and can be conceptualised as the developing capacity of the individual to delay gratification, inhibit impulses, and ultimately to learn.

A mounting number of studies have confirmed that the ability to delay gratification predicts future academic success, life management and health (e.g. Mischel et al., 1988; Mischel et al., 1989). It develops along with the maturation of the prefrontal areas that enable stress response regulation and guidance for the individual's actions (Luerssen et al., 2015). The ability to delay gratification is intertwined with the development of executive functions, which is the ability to control and focus attention, as well as inhibit inappropriate and impulsive responses. Executive functions play critical roles in predicting children's long-term outcomes, and success in school and in their social-emotional competence. Executive function abilities strengthen significantly throughout early childhood and therefore the years before primary school are crucial for practising these abilities. Executive functions allow children to attend appropriately to everyday activities and to participate, remember information, inhibit distractors and persist towards goals, all of which demonstrate successful stress response regulation. The characteristics of executive functions are positively related to social competence, reading, mathematic and linguistic abilities, and have been shown to improve the ability to remain focused and process detailed situations more accurately.

Stress response regulation, delayed gratification and executive function skills are known to show rapid growth in early childhood (Sturge-Apple et al., 2016). Preschool environments provide the opportunity to challenge and thus give the possibility for growth. In these environments children face the highest demands in regard to regulating themselves and addressing the various challenges presented. However, the elements of stress response regulation, delayed gratification or executive function have not been consistently taught in educational environments. The emphasis has, in some respects, been on pre-academic skills and behavioural management. Behavioural management has often been based on misunderstandings of the biological roots of the behaviour and thus the ways to intervene have tended to be based on discipline. In these cases, children's behaviour has not been understood through the lens of stress response regulation. This is a loss. In the globalised, swiftly changing, pluralistic and information-rich world, which offers multiple possibilities for creativity and self-guided learning, there is a risk that some children will be excluded. Self-guidance needs continuous executive functions and is a developmental ability that comes with a maturing stress-regulation system. This is essential for a fluid adaptation to changing situations, the maintenance of curiosity and interest in further learning, as well as for the acquisition of emotional and social abilities that support resilience in the face of stress. With the aim to prevent social and academic exclusion there thus should be much more understanding and sensitivity when encountering children with a diversity of backgrounds and regulative abilities (Gunnar and Fisher, 2006).

Pedagogical sensitivity

Human beings have a primary interest in other people. They are born with capacities to notice, assess relations and undertake sympathetic intentions towards others. On grounds of interpersonal neurobiology, the basic feelings of pleasure arise from engagement. Connections with others, full of feelings of belonging, reflect a positive balance of stress response regulation. During these moments, integrative brain functioning and resilient development are made possible. Inevitably, there are breaches in relations; children, as well as adults, are occasionally driven to quarrel because of conflicting desires, aims and opinions. Breaches are biologically alarming, causing accelerated stress responses. There is nothing wrong with this as long as the responses are regulated. For children who are struggling with regulation the adult's co-regulation is crucial. The adult's responsibility is to initiate a reconnection. That reconnection is calming and relaxing, and it restores the ability to listen, understand, think, and to be with others in a flexible manner (Sajaniemi et al., 2012).

Social exclusion is a great developmental risk factor for children and adolescents. Up to 10% of children and young people in Finland, for example, are at potential risk of social exclusion (Sajaniemi et al., 2013). This statistic is a human catastrophe and a tremendous loss of human potential for society. Exclusion is the accumulated experience of being left out, without the possibility to be seen, heard and understood. Based on preliminary findings, the signs of social exclusion can be recognised already in toddler groups (Sajaniemi et al., 2013). Both overactive and underactive stress-sensitive systems increase the risk through behaviour that jeopardises peer relations. For example, children who are withdrawing are sometimes seen as temperamentally shy, and on the basis of respect for individuality, they are left without support to join their peers. Further, peers are not necessarily willing to play with compulsive or defiant children. These children wish to be with others, however their unregulated stress responses have hindered the development of social abilities.

QUESTIONS FOR REFLECTION

1. On reflection, what opportunities do childhood education and care settings have for boosting holistic well-being and for opening pathways for lifelong learning?

2. Is it the adult's responsibility to interact with children in a way that helps them to regulate stress responses, develop resilience and extinguish maladaptive forms of behaviour? And if so, how can this be achieved?

3. Early education is a powerful tool in shaping the brain towards resilience and future achievements for children from non-privileged socio-economic backgrounds. How can the practitioner ensure quality in this respect?

4. How can practitioners support children to regulate their stress response, delay gratification or employ executive functions in educational environments?

SUMMARY

The fundamental value of the educational system should be to offer an experience of inclusion to all children. It should organise itself to accommodate the individually different developmental and biological needs of children – one size never fits all. Various needs generated by changing situations are not the basis of diagnoses. The breaking of regulation is not the fault of the child, but is the shortcoming of the recognition of biological and emotional signals by adults and their responses to them. Children signal their inner state continuously and search for answers that support positive feelings and help to manage negative ones. Education professionals should sensitise their senses, noticing signals from children while keeping group functioning as a priority. Pedagogically sensitive professionals can deliberately utilise warmth of expression and attuned oversight. Through their own expressions they can create a safe environment, which dampens overactive stress responses and helps the children to use their vagal brake. They can heavily support stress regulation through interpersonal engagement.

End of chapter glossary

- **Hypothalamus–Pituitary–Adrenal (HPA) axis** is a complex set of direct influences on three glands, in response to the external environment and internal monitoring, resulting in a gradual response to stress involving the production of hormones.
- **Neuroception** describes how neural circuits distinguish whether situations are safe or dangerous.
- **Stress response regulation** describes how the body prepares to protect itself against external threats, for example stress.
- **Sympatho–Adrenal–Medullary (SAM) axis** involves an immediate physiological response, including increased heartbeat and sweating palms, to the external environment and internal monitoring, involving nerves and resulting in a quick response to stress.
- The **vagal brake** inhibits, at the level of the heart, the strong response of the sympathetic nervous system to situations of stress, moderating reactive states of behaviour.
- The **ventral component of the vagal nerve** (VCC) activates the social engagement system, involving mechanisms of signalling and communication.

Further reading suggestions

Sajaniemi, N., Suhonen, E., Kontu, E., Lindholm, H. and Hirvonen, A. (2012) Stress reactivity of six-year-old children involved in challenging tasks, *Early Child Development and Care*, 182 (2):175-189.

Siegel, D.J. (2012) *The Developing Mind: How Relationships and the Brain Interact to Shape Who We Are* (2nd edition). New York: Guilford.

References

Blair, C. (2010) Stress and the development of self-regulation in context, *Child Development Perspectives*, 4 (3): 181–188.

Bright, M.A., Frick, J.E., Out, D. and Granger, D.A. (2014) Individual differences in the cortisol and salivary a-Amylase awakening responses in early childhood: relations to age, sex, and sleep, *Developmental Psychobiology*, 56 (6): 1300–1315.

Campbell, F.A., Conti, C., Heckman, J.J., Moon, S.H., Pinto, R., Pungello, E. and Pan, Y. (2014) Early childhood investments substantially boost adult health, *Science*, 343 (6178): 1478–1485.

Campbell, F.A., Pungello, E., Miller-Johnson, S., Burchinal, M.R. and Ramey, C. (2001) The development of cognitive and academic abilities: growth curves from an early childhood experiment, *Developmental Psychology*, 37: 231–244.

Doom, J.R. and Gunnar, M. (2014) Stress physiology and developmental psychopathology: past, present and future, *Developmental Psychopathology*, 25: 2–26.

Dougherty, L.R., Tolep, M.R., Bufferd, S.J., Olino, T.M., Dyson, M., Traditi, J., Rose, S., Carlson, G.A. and Klein, D.N. (2013) Preschool anxiety disorders: comprehensive assessment of clinical, demographic, temperamental, familial, and life stress correlates, *Journal of Clinical Child and Adolescent Psychology*, 42: 577–589.

Erel, O., Oberman, Y. and Yirmiya, N. (2000) Maternal versus nonmaternal care and seven domains of children's development, *Psychological Bulletin*, 126: 727–747.

Gunnar, M.R. and Fisher P.A. (2006) The Early Experience Stress Prevention Network: bringing basic research on early experience and stress neurobiology to bear on preventive interventions for neglected and maltreated children, *Development and Psychopathology*, 18: 651–677.

Herman, J.P. and Cullinan, W.E. (1997) Neurocircuitry of stress: central control of the hypo-thalamo–pituitary–adrenocortical axis, *Trends Neuroscience*, 20: 78–84.

Hermida, M.J., Segretin, M.S., Prats, L.M., Fracchia, J.A., Colombo, J.A. and Lipina, S.J. (2015) Cognitive neuroscience, developmental psychology, and education: interdisciplinary development of an intervention for low socioeconomic status kindergarten children, *Trends in Neuroscience and Education*, 4: 15–25.

Hill-Soderlund, A.L., Holochwost, S.J., Willoughby, M.T., Granger, D.A., Gariepy, J., Mills-Koonce, R.W. and Cox, M.J. (2015) The developmental course of salivary alpha-amylase and cortisol from 12 to 36 months: relations with early poverty and later behaviour problems. *Psychoneuroendochrinology*, 52: 311–323.

Hotulainen, R., Sajaniemi, N., Suhonen, E. and Thuneberg, H. (2014) Changes and stability in daily cortisol values and their correlation to attention measured in a prolonged working task among Finnish six-year-old children, *Journal of Child and Adolescent Behavior*, 2 (5): 8–16.

Johnson, M.H., Jones, E.J. and Gliga, T. (2015) Brain adaptation and alternative developmental trajectories, *Development and Psychopathology*, 27: 425–442.

Koss, K., Mlinerb, S.B., Donzellab, B. and Gunnar, M.B. (2016) Early adversity, hypocortisolism, and behaviour problems at school-entry: a study of internationally adopted children, *Psychoneuroendocrinology*, 66: 31–38.

Luerssen, A., Gyurak, A., Ayduk, O., Wendelken, C. and Bunge, S. (2015) Delay of gratification in childhood linked to cortical interactions with the nucleus accumbens, *Social Cognitive and Affective Neuroscience*, 10 (12): 1769–1776.

McClelland, M.M, Morrison, F.J. and Holmes, D.L. (2000) Children at risk for early academic problems: the role of learning-related social skills, *Early Childhood Research Quarterly*, 15 (3): 307–329.

Meaney, M. (2010) Epigenetics and the biological definition of gene x environment interactions, *Child Development*, 81 (1): 41–79.

Mischel, W., Shoda, Y. and Peake, P.K. (1988) The nature of adolescent competencies predicted by preschool delay of gratification, *Journal of Personality and Social Psychology*, 54: 687–696.

Mischel, W., Shoda, Y. and Rodriguez, M.L. (1989) Delay of gratification in children, *Science*, 244: 933–938.

Nater, U.M. and Rothleder, N. (2009) Salivary alpha-amylase as a non-invasive biomarker for the sympathetic nervous system: current state of research, *Psychoneuroendocrinology*, 34: 486–496.

Nelson, B.W., Parker, S.C. and Siegel, D.J. (2014) 'Interpersonal Neurobiology, Mindsight, and the Triangle of Well-being: The Mind, Relationships and the Brain'. In E. Tronick, B. Perry and K. Brandt (eds), *Infant & Early Childhood Mental Health*. Washington, DC: American Psychiatric Publishing.

Paulus, F., Backes, A., Sander, C., Weber, M. and von Gontard, A. (2015) Anxiety disorders and behavioural inhibition in preschool children: a population-based study, *Child Psychiatry Human Development*, 46: 150–157.

Petresco, S., Anselmi, L., Santos, I., Barros, A., Fleitlich-Bilyk, B., Barros, F. and Matijasevich, A. (2004) Prevalence and comorbidity of psychiatric disorders among 6-year-old children: 2004 Pelotas Birth Cohort, *Social Psychiatry and Psychiatric Epidemiology*, 49: 975–983.

Porges, S.W. (2004) Neuroception: a subconscious system for detecting threats and safety, *Zero to Three*, 24 (5): 19–24.

Porges, S.W. (2007) The polyvagal perspective, *Biological Psychology*, 74 (2): 116–143.

Repo, L. and Sajaniemi, N. (2015) Prevention of bullying in early educational settings: pedagogical and organizational factors related to bullying, *European Early Childhood Education Research* Journal, 23 (4): 461–475.

Sajaniemi, N., Suhonen, E., Kontu, E., Lindholm, H. and Hirvonen, A. (2012) Stress reactivity of six-year-old children involved in challenging tasks, *Early Child Development and Care*, 182 (2):175–189.

Sajaniemi, N., Suhonen, E., Kontu, E., Rantanen, P., Lindholm, H. and Hirvonen, A. (2011) Children's cortisol patterns and the quality of the early learning environment, *European Early Childhood Education Research Journal*, 19 (1): 45–62.

Sajaniemi, N., Suhonen, E., Nislin, M. and Mäkelä, J. (2015) *Stress Regulation: The Core of Interaction, Development and Learning*. PS-kustannus, Jyväskylä.

Sajaniemi, N., Suhonen, E., Törmänen, M., Hotulainen, R., Alijoki, A. and Nislin, M. (2013) Demographic factors, temperament and the quality of preschool environment as predictors of daily cortisol changes among the Finnish six year old children, *European Early Childhood Research Journal*, 22 (2): 286–306.

Sajaniemi, N., Suhonen, E. and Sims, M. (2011) A preliminary exploration of children's physiological arousal levels in regular preschool settings, *Australian Journal of Early Childhood*, 36 (3): 91–99.

Siegel, D. (2010) *Mindsight*. London: Random House.

Siegel, D. (2012) The *Developing Mind: How Relationships and the Brain Interact to Shape Who We Are* (2nd edition). New York: Guilford.

Sturge-Apple, M.L., Suor, J.H., Davies, P.T., Cicchetti, D., Skibo, M. and Rogosch, F.A. (2016) Vagal tone and children's delay of gratification: differential sensitivity in resource-poor and resource-rich environments, *Psychological Science*, 27 (6): 885–893.

Suhonen, E., Sajaniemi, N., Alijoki, A. and Nislin, M. (2016) Children's biological givens, stress responses, language and cognitive abilities and family background after entering kindergarten in toddlerhood, *Early Child Development and Care*. Online. pp. 1–14.

Sylva, K., Melhuish, E., Sammons, P., Siraj-Blatchford, I. and Taggart, B. (2010) *Early Childhood Matters: Evidence from the Effective Pre-school and Primary Education Project*. Abingdon: Routledge.

Syrjämäki, M.E., Sajaniemi, N.K., Suhonen, E.A., Alijoki, A.A.K. and Nislin, M.A. (2016) Enhancing peer interaction: an aspect of a high quality learning environment in Finnish Early Childhood Special Education, *European Journal of Special Needs Education*. Online: DOI: 10.1080/08856257.2016.1240342.

7

THE POLITICAL CHILD

SUE CRONIN, GED MULHANEY AND MICHELLE PEARSON

CHAPTER OBJECTIVES

- To explore the implications of politics and policies and, in particular, English policies on Early Years provision in England.
- To discuss the impact of the political discourse of 'readiness' on young children and those who are involved in their education and development.

> If we want our children to succeed at school, go on to university or into an apprenticeship and thrive in later life, we must get it right in the early years. If we want to use the talents of parents, and particularly mothers, to the full, we must ensure there is enough high quality childcare available. (DfE, 2013)

The above quote is taken from a policy report undertaken by the UK Coalition government of Conservative and Liberal Democrats who oversaw Early Years Education from 2010 to 2015. The sentiment and rhetoric still remain true today under the present Conservative government; the desire for academic, and thus economic, success for future generations is at the forefront of Early Years policy initiatives. Closely allied to this is the accompanying political drive to increase parental, and in particular, maternal employment rates and the associated economic benefits in terms of potential increases in taxation and reduced welfare expenditure. The sense of urgency in ensuring the development of high-quality childcare has continued to increase, and the focus on being 'ready' to succeed underpins the political discourse of the current UK government. This chapter sets out to consider some of the implications for children and practitioners as a result of the political push to ensure the children's readiness to enter formal education.

Current landscape

The Department for Education introduced an entitlement to 15 hours of free childcare per week for all 3 and 4 year-olds in England in September 2010. There was an expectation that this would provide early education for children and the associated developmental benefits, in particular targeting the most deprived children to ensure 'school readiness'. In 2013 the Department extended the offer of free childcare to include 2 year-olds from disadvantaged families, as this was becoming an increasing area of interest (Field, 2010). This free childcare could take place in a wide range of settings, such as playgroups, preschools, nursery schools, nursery classes in primary schools, Children's Centres or with childminders. In 2015–16 there were approximately 105,000 childcare providers in England. The Department oversaw the delivery of this childcare, setting the overall policy for free childcare including the Early Years Foundation Stage (a framework which sets standards for the learning, development and care of children from birth to 5 years-old). Funding to implement the policy was then devolved to Local Authorities. In 2015–16 the Department gave £2.7 billion to Local Authorities, with 1.5 million children taking up free childcare places (House of Commons Committee of Public Accounts, 2016). The Local Authorities were then charged with the responsibility of ensuring sufficient places for the funded hours and the appropriate allocation of money to providers. They are legally required to provide information to help parents find an appropriate place for their child, and they are also expected to give support and training to these providers as part of their responsibility to ensure the childcare is of high quality. However, although providers must register with Ofsted, which inspects childcare settings to ensure they deliver good-quality education and care, they can choose whether to offer free childcare, and similarly, parents are free to choose which provider or combination of providers they select and how many hours to access.

The rhetoric of readiness

Part of the political imperative for increased resourcing is the notion of school readiness. The rhetoric of readiness for education has become a dominant discourse in English education policy and, it could be argued, dominates the holistic emotional, social and intellectual needs of the individual child. The emphasis on economic success is not unique to England, as Jarvis et al. describe: 'Governments of all political persuasions are often particularly interested in the fate of their nation's children, and not always for the most charitable reasons, being inclined to view them as projects for a collective national future rather than as individuals: the children as human capital agenda' (2016: 113).

That there is a global consensus around the critical importance of experiences and the education provided for young children is incontestable (Anderson, 2008; Corak et al., 2012; Bertram and Pascal, 2014). What is contestable however is the underlying philosophic and ideological beliefs manifest in the political stances which shape these formative experiences. Globally, politicians may reflect different views and degrees of interest in what the experiences for young children should be, but the general direction is unified. The overriding hegemony is socially imagined in terms of neoliberal marketisation and global competitiveness (Rizvi and Lingard, 2010). The groundwork for an effective workforce begins with preschool experiences; foundations for a country's economic success are forged in nurseries and informal childcare settings. Additionally, in England perhaps more than most countries, these differences concerning the best way to educate the young are accentuated at a cross-party level. Policies are driven by the timeframe of elections, with each new politician entering the education arena keen to make their mark, at best simply revising policy but more often reversing the policy direction of those previously holding office, leading to instability and uncertainty for those tasked with managing the provision. The fluctuations in party politics frame the prevailing priorities, swinging from promotion of equality of opportunity through central funding, to greater competition and devolved budgets, encouraging targeted resourcing to focus on improved outcomes (Halavaara-Robertson and Hill, 2014).

The closure of Sure Start centres is one example of such a political policy reversal. Sure Start centres were originally opened by Labour in 1998 and designed to help parents in the community, providing a central hub for healthcare, childcare, education and family support. Under the subsequent Coalition government there was a swing away from centre funding towards more targeted services for families who were most in need. However, as a result there was a potential reduction in parenting services for those families who would only be seen through such universal, levelled services. A census report by the charity 4Children (2015), itself now a defunct victim of the fragility of financial changes in children's services, noted a 35% fall in spending on Children's Centres from £1.2 billion in 2010 to £740 million in 2015. The austerity measures and resulting government cuts on Local Authority budgets had resulted in the closure of 99 centres in the first six months of 2015, a marked increase on the 83 closures across the whole of the previous year.

School readiness

According to Shallwani, school readiness is a socially and culturally constructed notion which should be focused on 'a child's experience at the micro level and ignores macro level and systemic factors ... and sees childhood as a time for preparation for adulthood and young children needing to be made ready for school' (2009: 4). This notion of school readiness suggests a different experience in different social contexts, thus lying in opposition to a political desire for greater uniformity of experience. Additionally, the research of Dockett et al. (2010) suggests that different stakeholders also interpret readiness differently. They found that teachers tended to focus on a child's ability to adapt to the school specific context. In contrast parents focused on the child's interpersonal and social adjustment ('Are they happy and making friends?': the question that all parents ask whatever the context of the school or child). Children themselves tended to focus on understanding the rules, doing the right thing, and making friends. The image that children have of themselves, as learners in the very earliest years, does impact on their continuing academic and social success (Melhuish et al., 2008; Sylva et al., 2008). Children who experience similar environments and expectations at home and school are likely to find the transition into school an easier process. This fact has developed into a focus, resulting in the development of dialogue with parents and in practitioners trying to influence the Home Learning Environment. UNICEF (2012) have also highlighted that there is a need for the school to be ready for the child and family, as well as the child being ready for school. They state that 'child-friendly schools are child-centred and focus on characteristics that are most beneficial for children's holistic development and comprehensive learning. These schools seek to involve the child's environment – family and community – thereby linking the three dimensions of school readiness' (2012: 7).

Again, this creates tension with the notion of having all children at the same level of readiness, in particular academic readiness, at the start of formal schooling. The political pressure is to forward think, to look ahead, rather than allowing room for early childhood to be seen as a distinct, valuable phase that is meaningful to the child, the family and the community in its own right. Instead of a focus on the image of the child as a unique child, a competent and capable learner, there is a danger in the emergence of a deficiency model focusing on what is missing for the next stage. The school readiness agenda influences the direction of teaching, learning and pedagogy, and for many narrows the curriculum experiences in these key years. Studies of successful preschools by Sylva et al. (2008) and Melhuish et al. (2008) indicate that preschools which promote activities for parents and children to engage in together are likely to be most beneficial for young children. This has implications for strategies that seek to help disadvantaged children start school with more academic skills and maintain their educational achievement.

CASE STUDY 7.1   EXPLORING THE SOCIAL PEDAGOGICAL APPROACH

An example of a school readiness project that focused on an inclusive and creative approach to encouraging social skills, independence, communication and learning skills is the work undertaken by Liverpool Children's Centres and the Tate Gallery in Liverpool.

The project provided a way of working together collaboratively with local cultural organisations, artists, Children's Centres, PVIs, practitioners, parents and children. It involved parents, practitioners and artists in learning and delighting in the children's responses. The approach was based on the principles of Reggio Emilia in that the artist worked with the children to explore the local environment, scaffolding experiences to offer a chance for children to use their senses to respond in a variety of ways and providing an atelier environment that used a wide range of materials. Making the play-based learning visible in the interactions with all the children and adults involved provided an environment for creative learning together, leading to the extension of experiences, language and communication.

(Continued)

(Continued)

During the project the children demonstrated that they were competent learners, making connections in their learning to represent their ideas and responses. Evidence from the project indicated high levels of well-being and involvement that were displayed by the children in active, creative thinking and talking. They displayed social interaction, listening and attention, understanding, speaking, drawing and mark making in line with appropriate age-related expectations, helping to show school readiness.

Poverty, politics and the Early Years

The politics of poverty and social disadvantage are particularly critical in the Early Years arena, as we shall see in Chapter 9. Closing the socio-economic gaps between the disadvantaged child and their peers continues to exercise the minds of professionals and politicians alike. Inevitably, the challenge is tied to the problem of adequate funding and the resourcing levels required to address some of the increasing inequities and growing levels of poverty. The House of Commons Committee of Public Accounts report (2016) into free early years education and childcare noted that the Department for Education had made 'significant progress' towards the goal of ensuring all 3 and 4 year-olds benefit from 15 hours per week of free early years education and childcare. The report detailed that 94% of 3 year-olds and 99% of 4 year-olds took up a funded place in 2015. This was a positive statistic but the numbers from the most disadvantaged backgrounds were less impressive, with only 58% taking up their additional hours entitlement. Part of the rationale for the free childcare entitlement, as one of the Department for Education's flagship policies, has been to address the educational achievement gap between disadvantaged children and their peers. They acknowledge the poverty–achievement gap is an acute problem facing the country and its future potential for further success. As the report by the Institute of Health Equity states:

> Rising unemployment, poorer working conditions, depressed incomes and an inability to pay for decent housing and basic needs will all increase negative mental and physical health outcomes across the social gradient and especially for more vulnerable groups. Those unemployed for long periods of time will be more likely to be unemployed in the future, and higher levels of parental stress will lead to worse outcomes for many of the children of this generation. (Bowers et al., 2014: 9)

The present government has set out to address these issues through the introduction of the Early Years National Funding Formula (EYNFF), and at the same time introducing an increase from 15 to 30 hours of childcare funding by 2017. The DfE states in its consultation response document:

All three and four year olds are already entitled to 15 hours a week of free early learning. Take-up is high, at 95%, and the quality of provision continues to improve, with 85% of children taking up their place in a 'good' or 'outstanding' setting. The government will deliver this new commitment through local authorities, as it does for the existing 15 hours. (DfE, 2016: 4)

The pledge to ensure a high rate of take-up may be seen as an attempt to address previous concerns around take-up rates, particularly by families who could most benefit from the additional support. Initially, this may seem a positive development but presently the services for early years (0–5 years-old) consist of a diverse mix of public, private and voluntary providers. None of these providers are compulsory and they operate in a competitive marketplace, forced to do what is needed to ensure they attract sufficient funding from parents and carers to stay in business. This often makes the poorer families less attractive as they will not necessarily have additional funds available to top up the free childcare with additional hours. According to the House of Commons Committee of Public Accounts report (2016), many private and voluntary providers state that the current levels of funding for free childcare are insufficient to cover their costs. For many families the economic challenge of meeting additional costs proves a sufficient barrier to realising the resource of good childcare. Worryingly the report cites evidence from a voluntary children's organisation, Gingerbread, who had received complaints from parents that many childcare providers were making the uptake of paid additional hours a requirement to access the free hours. Although this should not be a condition of access to the entitlement, the regulation of this is patchy according to the Local Authority. Thus the EYNFF may be a simplistic solution to a complex problem. The House of Commons report from the Committee of Public Accounts summarises the main tensions:

> Parents remain confused about the free entitlement and how to access free childcare; half of parents with children under four are not sure what help they could get with childcare costs. The quality of the information provided by local authorities' family information services to parents varies significantly, and only 30% of parents are even aware of this service. There is a risk that not enough providers will be willing to provide the additional 15 hours of free childcare that the Department will offer working families from September 2017. (2016: 3)

The funding of the EYNFF policy gives all nurseries in the sector – private, public and voluntary – the same standardised single base rate payment. In evidence to the Public Accounts Committee, the Department for Education stated the policy was a 'result of history rather than maths' (2016: 27; Question 91). In reality the combination of the national and local funding formulae has led to a profoundly concerning level of difference in the amount of funding given to providers by different local authorities. As a result, the very nursery provision that supports increased life chances for children in more disadvantaged areas will lose out, and therefore potentially the very families the government wants to target may not benefit from the EYNFF single base rate.

Where should the early years child start to get ready?

In addition to the management of EYS funding, there is a pressing imperative for government to consider the quality and the suitability of providers. The variation of providers offering Early Years education and childcare is not consistent across local authorities and even within local authorities. In areas of social deprivation, the choice and range of flexible childcare and education available, for reasons including those outlined above, may be limited. Many private and voluntary providers may be unable to operate as a viable business given the constraints on funding, and many schools are not necessarily equipped to step in to fill the gap. This becomes an even more acute problem if the children have additional needs, such as SEN. In his submission to the Public Accounts Committee, Neil Leitch (Chief Executive, Pre-School Learning Alliance) outlined the tensions:

> I think it is difficult to deny that providers in areas of deprivation will suffer harder. They have more and more cases to deal with involving children with special needs, or children in care or on the at-risk register and so on, so there is more of a workload. We have to attend more and more meetings outside the conventional environment. There is no funding to pay for that and no consideration in terms of average rates. (2016: 4; Question 10)

Implicit in this evidence is the recognition that Early Years provision is complex and requires expertise and skills that must be appropriate if it is to be of the highest quality. Many vulnerable groups of children face additional barriers to their development, as we have seen in Chapter 5, and these require time and expert intervention to ensure they are able to make good progress. Many of the private and voluntary providers would see the moral imperative to address the multiple barriers. However, for some this may be too big an ask – the recognition of the additional work to ensure quality experiences is certainly not realised in monetary terms, and the extra workload could be the tipping-point for a business.

Ullucci and Howard (2016) have outlined the mythologies surrounding the education of the poor. They suggest that during their time as teachers and teacher educators they have come to recognise persistent myths and claims about children in poverty. All of these simplify the interrelationships and many factors that face families struggling to survive in areas of deprivation. One such myth they suggest is that of the 'Educability myth', where it is taken for granted that children in poverty are broken and defined by what they cannot do (Ullucci and Howard, 2016: 177). The idea that poor children are not particularly smart or school-ready has been evident and prominent in the rhetoric of many government ministers and politicians.

Michael Gove, as Secretary of State for Education, stated that:

If children arrive in school unable to sit, listen and learn and then disrupt the learning of others then lives begin already blighted. The difficulty they have in dealing with children who arrive in reception class totally unprepared to learn. Which is why we [government] are intervening. (2015)

Sir Michael Wilshaw went on to say:

Let me be clear: What the poorest children need is to be taught and well taught from the age of two ... Children who are at risk of falling behind need particular help. And it remains my view that schools are often best placed to deliver this. (2015)

The privileging of the primary school as the most appropriate setting for early years education is contested. The general secretary of the Association of Teachers and Lecturers, Dr Mary Bousted, argued:

While schools do offer many benefits, including the potential for an easier transition into reception and beyond, they are not necessarily geared up to support very young children. And teachers are not necessarily trained to teach two-year-olds. (Bousted quoted in Richardson, 2015)

Workforce policy in England – encouraging high quality in the early years?

Research (Mathers and Sylva, 2007; Mathers et al., 2011; Nutbrown, 2012) into improving children's life chances indicates that children need access to high-quality early years provision, and that requires a qualified and competent workforce who are able to work with the youngest learners effectively to maximise learning opportunities. The factors identified as constituting high-quality provision include the importance of the leadership in the setting being at graduate level, with the highest impact resulting from a trained professional working with and planning the curriculum for children aged 30 months to 5 years-old (Mathers et al., 2011). The Nutbrown Review (2012), thus far, has not had the intended impact in terms of employment in the Early Years sector. It sets out to ensure that all staff have a minimum of a Level 3 qualification by 2022, but currently the sector is not bound statutorily to have graduate leaders or trained practitioners. This then perpetuates this oddly casual approach to recruitment in terms of some of the most important people in a young child's education and learning process. The previous commitment of the new Labour government to a graduate-led workforce has been watered down, from a graduate in every full daycare setting to the more nebulous commitment to a graduate-led (Level 6) provision. The NVQ Level 3 remains the basic qualification for staffing. The previous government's attempt at up-levelling professionalism through the system of the Early Years Practitioner (EYP) was effectively discredited, as practitioners were advised to gain recognised Qualified Teacher Status (QTS) in order to fulfil a graduate component of the qualification, thereby

undermining the credibility of the EYP design as a professional leadership qualification that focused on all aspects of leadership and management for quality
provision in the Early Years and Foundation stage.

This EYP qualification has subsequently been replaced with the equally controversial Early Years Teacher (EYT), which also appears to be failing to deliver a
credible qualification, in terms of status or pay, with the recognised Qualified
Teacher Status available for the rest of the teaching profession. Funding to study
the Early Years Teacher qualification is also fraught with difficulties in terms of
bursary awards and a lack of parity in terms of weighting with other postgraduate
qualifications, leading to a lack of involvement by many universities and providers.
It can be seen that the teacher who is based in the Early Years is given less value
economically, socially and culturally. This is at odds with the research which tells us
that these are some of the most significant growth learning stages in child development. As a result of these political decisions, and to some extent indecisions, to
rationalise the Early Years workforce, employment in the sector continues to be
characterised by a piecemeal and casual approach to the recruitment of some of the
most important people in a young child's education and learning process.

Measuring and testing – too much, too soon?

Running parallel to a recognition of the importance of the preschool experience
and its positive, long-term impact on a child's attainment, progress and social
behavioural development are the accountability agenda and pervading performa-
tivity culture. Readiness has to be measured and weighed to assure politicians that
progress is being made towards the up-skilling of tomorrow's workforce. This
translates currently into the main requirement of Early Years teachers in schools to
ensure that all children reach a Good Level of Development (GLD) by the end of
Reception and before they enter Year 1. The emphasis on GLD has changed to more
academically-driven outcomes in the years since 2014. A GLD is now achieved by
gaining the expected level in all three of the prime areas of Personal, Social and
Emotional Development, Physical Development, and Communication and
Language, combined with the specific areas of Literacy and Mathematics. The
more creative areas of Understanding the World and Expressive Arts and Design
no longer count towards an overall level, despite the EYFS curriculum stating that
there should be equal weighting in all areas of learning and development, mirroring the recently narrowed secondary curriculum with its increased focus on more
traditionally academic subjects. The expected levels have also changed over the last
few years and new assessment materials for literacy and mathematics outline
higher expectations for children in order to achieve expected levels of progress, in
line with changes to the National Curriculum.

When the GLD was introduced only 52% of children were achieving the necessary outcomes; today the number of children achieving a GLD has risen to 68%.
However, this rise may be a stronger indication that teachers are aware of the outcomes and focusing their teaching, learning and assessments accordingly to find
evidence of those outcomes. It could therefore potentially be seen that Biesta's

(2010) view that the 'anticipation of assessment' is creating conditions in which assessment is leading the curriculum content and reducing the complexity of learning and development.

CASE STUDY 7.2   EXPLORING ASSESSMENT

The following details the view of an Early Year's Moderator:

I have been a moderator for six years and in that time I have visited a wide range of schools. The last few years I have seen a change from a range of settings and styles to a more homogeneous approach. Learning environments seem to be very similar, with children from all areas and cultures being taught and learning the same despite differences.

The year the changes in maths and writing were introduced all the schools visited showed changes to their learning environments, linked to the maths or writing outcomes. Where once you would not have seen any provision, resources or examples of halving, doubling or sharing in a reception class when you visited to do moderation, this now took pride of place. Games indoors and outdoors were shown with pride as areas where children were able to show their skills in these areas, which just happened to now be part of the expected level for the end of EYFS.

In writing, reception children have to show evidence of producing long passages of writing in child-initiated contexts with no adult support. Staff had thus created areas for writing in every area of the indoors and outdoors; working walls with examples of a range of genres to provoke writing appeared across the settings.

The year the changes appeared every school visited had examples which were very similar to the exemplification materials, consisting of children supposedly deciding to write instructions for making models, baking or planting, or writing out favourite fairy tales. Often there were whole-class 'child-initiated' examples, which were questionable.

Over the last few years the changes in assessment seemed to be leading the provision and learning opportunities. There is pressure on EYFS classes to be preparing children from the very beginning of the year to be ready to undertake a prescriptive, formal curriculum by term 3 of Reception, so that children gain not only the Early Learning Goals in Reception but also that these children are ready for Year 1 and the chance of attaining the inflated expected levels by being able to sit still, listen for long periods of time, be pliable, and respond to stimuli all day, everyday.

QUESTIONS FOR REFLECTION

1. What is your image and construct of a child in the Early Years? How does this compare to the current political ideology?

2. Reflect on Case Study 7.1. What strategies would you use to create a dialogue to promote a shared understanding of being ready for school with all those involved in the process?

(Continued)

(Continued)

3. Reflect on your everyday practice. Do you make all families feel welcome? How do you take account of and celebrate the distinct social, cultural and geographical features of the community that your children come from?

4. Do you think that high-quality early education is crucial in countering the effects of socio-economic disadvantage?

SUMMARY

The increase in more formal structured approaches in early years provision, with a linear hierarchy of skills designed to promote a pre-primary model, is contradictory to the neurological, social and developmental structures that would best be served by a later transition point to formal education. Garnering a social pedagogical approach to Early Years appears to elicit better results in terms of long-term educational attainment, as seen in the Nordic countries of Finland and Norway. The politicisation of early years education and care in the United Kingdom, however, represents a collective failure to focus on the here and now for this very important stage of childhood.

End of chapter glossary

- **Policy** details a principle of action expected by an organisation.
- **Politics** includes the activities involved with the governance of a country.
- **School readiness** is a measure of how prepared a child is to thrive in school.
- **Social pedagogical approaches** are based on principles concerned with the theory of holistic education and care.

Further reading

Halvaara-Robertson, L. and Hill, D. (2014) Policy and ideologies in schooling and Early Years education in England: implications for and impacts on leadership, management and equality, *Management in Education*, 28 (4): 167–174.

Nutbrown, C. (2012) *Foundations for Quality: The independent review of early years education and childcare qualifications*. Final Report. Available at www.gov.uk/government/uploads/system/uploads/attachment_data/file/175463/Nutbrown-Review.pdf (last accessed 16 December 2016).

References

Anderson, P. (2008) *Young Children's' Rights* (2nd edition). London: Jessica Kingsley.

Bertram, T. and Pascal, C. (2014) *Early Years Literature Review*. Centre for Research in Early Childhood. Available at www.early-education.org.uk/sites/default/files/CREC%20Early%20Years%20Lit%20Review%202014%20for%20EE.pdf (last accessed 16 December 2016).

Biesta, G. (2010) A new logic of emancipation: the methodology of Jacques Ranciere, *Educational Theory*, 60 (1): 39–59.

Bowers, A.P., Strelitz J., Allen J. and Donkin A. (2014) *An Equal Start: Improving Outcomes in Children's Centres: An Evidence Review.* London: UCL Institute of Health Equity.

4Children (2015) *Children's Centres Census 2015: A national overview of Children's Centres in 2015.* Available at www.4children.org.uk/Files/28082f59-4cb8-4116-a476-a536009 e5d05/Children_Centre_Census_2015.pdf (last accessed 28 March 2017).

Corak, M., Waldfogel, J., Washbrook, L., Ermisch, J., Vignoles, A., Jerrim, J., Vignoles, A. and Jerrim, J. (2012) *Social Mobility and Education Gaps in the Four Major Anglophone Countries: Research Findings for the Social Mobility Summit.* Available at www.sutton trust.com/researcharchive/social-mobility-education-gaps-four-major-anglophone-countries-research-findings-social-mobility-summit-london-2012/ (last accessed 23 October 2016).

Department for Education (DfE) (2013) Consultation on Early Education and Childcare Staff Deployment. Runcorn: CSDSD.

Department for Education (DfE) (2016) 30 hours free childcare entitlement: delivery model, *Government Consultation Response.* London: National Archives.

Dockett, S., Perry, B. and Kearney, E. (2010) School Readiness: What does it mean for indigenous children, families, schools and communities. Available at www.aihw.gov.au/ uploadedFiles/ClosingTheGap/Content/Publications/2010/ctg-ip02.pdf (last accessed 16 December 2016).

Field, F. (2010) The Foundation Years: Preventing poor children becoming poor adults. *The Report of the Independent Review on Poverty and Life Chances.* London: Crown.

Gove, M. (2015) HMI speech at the launch of Ofsted's early years report. Available at www. gov.uk/government/speeches/early-years-report-2015

Halvaara-Robertson, L. and Hill, D. (2014) Policy and ideologies in schooling and Early Years education in England: implications for and impacts on leadership, management and equality, *Management in Education*, 28 (4): 167–174.

House of Commons Committee of Public Accounts (2016) Entitlement to free early years education and childcare. *Fourth Report: HC224.* Available at www.publications. parliament.uk/pa/cm201617/cmselect/cmpubacc/224/22411.htm (last accessed 13 December 2016).

Jarvis, P., George, J., Holland, W. and Doherty, J. (2016) 'Principles in Childcare and Education'. In P. Jarvis, J. George, W. Holland and J. Doherty (eds), *The Complete Companion for Teaching and Leading Practice in the Early Years.* New York: Routledge.

Mathers, S., Ranns, H., Karemaker, A., Moody, A., Sylva, K., Graham, J. and Siraj-Blatchford I. (2011) Evaluation of the Graduate Leader Fund Final Report. *Research Report DfE-RR144.* Available at www.education.gov.uk/publications/eOrderingDownload/ DFE-RR144.pdf (last accessed 16 December 2016).

Mathers, S. and Sylva, K. (2007) National Evaluation of the Neighbourhood Nurseries Initiative: The Relationship Between Quality and Children's Behavioural Development. *Research Report DfE-SSU/2007/FR/022.* Available at www.education.gov.uk/publications/ eOrderingDownload/SSU-2007-FR-022.pdf (last accessed 29 March 2017).

Melhuish E., Phan, M., Sylva, K., Sammons, P., Siraj-Blatchford, I. and Taggart, B. (2008) Effects of the home learning environment and preschool center experience upon literacy and numeracy development in early primary school, *Journal of Social Issues*, 64 (1): 95–114.

Nutbrown, C. (2012) Foundations for Quality: The independent review of early years education and childcare qualifications. *Final Report.* Available at www.gov.uk/government/ uploads/system/uploads/attachment_data/file/175463/Nutbrown-Review.pdf (last accessed 29 March 2017).

Richardson, H. (2015) Poorest pupils 'should start school aged two'. *BBC News*. Available at www.bbc.co.uk/news/education-33476052 (last accessed 29 March 2017).

Rizvi, F. and Lingard, B. (2010) *Globalizing Education Policy.* London: Routledge.

Shallwani, S. (2009) The Social Construction of School Readiness. *CIES Conference.* Paper presented at the Annual Conference of the Comparative and International Education Society, University of Toronto.

Sylva, K., Melhuish, E., Sammons, P., Siraj-Blatchford, I. and Taggart, B. (2008) *Final Report from the Primary Phase: Pre-school, School and Family Influences on Children's Development during Key Stage 2 (7–11).* Nottingham: DCSF RR 061.

Ullucci, K. and Howard, T. (2016) Pathologizing the poor: implications for preparing teachers to work in high-poverty schools, *Urban Education*, 2: 170–193.

UNICEF (2012) *School Readiness: A Conceptual Framework.* New York: UN Children's Fund.

Wilshaw, M. (2015) Her Majesty's Chief Inspector Sir Michael Wilshaw's speech at the launch of Ofsted's early years report 2015. Available at www.gov.uk/government/speeches/early-years-report-2015 (last accessed 29 March 2017).

8

THE NATURAL CHILD

HARRIET PATTISON

CHAPTER OBJECTIVES

- To consider influences on cultural constructions of childhood.

- To think about how different understandings and constructions of nature play into ideas about childhood.

- To consider how ideas in society cross-fertilise through subject matters.

'All contemporary approaches to the study of childhood are clearly committed to the view that childhood is not a natural phenomenon and cannot properly be understood as such' (Jenks, 2005: 6). As Jenks emphatically reminds us, the present-day view of childhood is overwhelmingly that childhood is not natural but is, as he goes on to argue, a social construct. This means that our knowledge of children is shaped not by understandings inherent to the state of childhood but by much wider forces influencing our thinking. Beliefs about children – how they learn, how they grow, what they need and how to treat them – come not from general facts about children but from interpretations made through the contexts of, for example, politics, economics, culture, philosophy and religion. Given this, there seems little to pursue under the title of the 'natural child'. Instead, as Jenks argues, contemporary thought has moved on, leaving the natural child as a relegated piece of misguided history. However, in other circles, it seems that talk of the natural child has not abated and the linking of childhood to nature in various ways continues (Taylor, 2013). Rather than losing its grip the natural child appears to have an enduring appeal, and is perhaps even being reinvented for the 21st century.

To this end, the chapter explores two different understandings of the natural child and considers why the appeal of the natural, when it comes to thinking about childhood, somehow seems to refuse to go away, and is instead undergoing a makeover in current thinking. First, however, I shall turn to the question of the natural.

What is nature?

Since we are concerned with childhood and the child, the question 'what is the child?' is a common and rational starting-place. Understanding children and investigating children will generally start from observing and thinking about children. However, if the state of childhood is primarily a cultural construct, as Jenks (2005) is arguing, then wondering what children are needs to be directed through the lens of culture – the political, the economic, the religious, the popular, the social. If it is within these perspectives that the construction of the child takes place, then understanding the child must also be located inside such views. So considering the natural child is a call to think about nature as much as about children. What do we mean when we talk about nature and the natural? What is it about nature that makes us want to link it with children? How can unpacking our ideas about nature help us to understand how we interpret childhood?

The subject of nature is one with a long philosophical pedigree. Since the time of the ancient Greeks, philosophers have worried away at the nature of nature. It was a particular interest for Aristotle (Bodnar, 2012) and philosophers continue to explore this today, very often with little in the way of agreement (Lamb, 1996). A major sticking-point is how should nature best be distinguished from culture, its oft-cited counterpart? The question itself is a reflection of long-standing dualisms in western thought, which divide the world into binary oppositions such as good and evil, child and adult, nature and culture. Not only has this kind of structuralist thinking been widely influential in philosophical thought, but its presence is also felt in numerous everyday practices and institutions. A ready-to-hand example would be the arrangements of western universities where science and arts or humanities are typically separated from each other, not least because they are projected as dealing with quite different kinds of 'truths' (Barnes, 1974). In terms of our philosophical heritage, defining nature through its opposition to culture feels like an obvious move. But it is also one which throws up difficulties.

There are instances in which nature and culture do not seem to separate easily, for example in the case of human beings where it seems that we are self-evidently both natural beings and, equally obviously, cultural beings. The debate becomes even more intractable when applied to children, where the respective influences of nature and nurture continue to fuel much live debate (see for example Eagly and Wood, 2013). On one level children are unmistakably natural beings. Indeed, it seems impossible even for the sociologist to transcend the biological basis of early childhood. The child is an embodied, physical fact, and her capabilities and development are necessarily constrained within, ordered by, and dependent on that fact. However, this biological base, argue the sociologists, is interpreted and shaped through the influence of culture (Prout, 2008). Illustrative of this intertwining is, for example, the 4Children *What to Expect, When? Guide* (2015) on learning and development, which makes widespread reference to child development interpreted through the use of books, toys, cutlery and cultural practices of talking to and interacting with children. Children at different stages of development are expected to react differently to stimuli such as toys or being called by name. They are expected to respond to cultural artefacts like their clothes, drinking cup or nappies in particular ways. Child development, both physical and mental, is understood through children's engagement with cultural objects and their collaboration in cultural practices. Not only are these reactions taken to be signs of development, but they also direct our understandings of child development so that our expectations of 'natural' child development are bound up with our particular cultural context. Yet the bias in this approach is made clear by the ethnographic record, which shows that much of this simply would not apply to many of the world's children who, for example, do not wear nappies, do not own toys, do not eat with cutlery, and may not even be named from birth (Lancy, 2015).

Documents such as the *4Children Guide* (2015) map an apparently natural course of development through cultural means, and thereby exemplify the way in which understanding childhood is caught in the tension of the nature–culture dichotomy. For this reason, the argument commonly distils down to a question of proportion: how much of the child is natural and how much is cultural? Prout (2008) documents what he calls the zig-zagging course which interpretations of childhood have taken, as academic understanding bounces between the poles of nature and culture. Yet these two are not in themselves fixed spaces divided by a clear boundary between which an interpretation of childhood can be placed. Before it can be determined whether the child is primarily natural or primarily cultural, it must first be decided what nature is, what culture is, and how to distinguish one from the other. Some kind of definition of nature needs to be agreed on. However there is no such agreement, and fuelled with fresh impetus from concerns such as climate change, the use of environmental resources and the protection of certain habitats and environments, this is a matter giving rise to a good deal of debate (Lamb, 1996; Castree and Braun, 1998; Demerritt, 2002). Like Aristotle, present-day philosophy has found that 'it remains unclear just what nature is' (Valkanova, 2015: 11).

What is certain, however, is that any clarification of this can only be achieved through cultural means. Only human understanding, expressed through human language, argument and judgement, can determine where the demarcation between nature and culture should fall. We can see this perhaps most clearly by thinking about societies which do not distinguish between nature and culture, thereby allowing quite different interpretations of what it is to be human to emerge (Descola, 2013). Nature and culture are aspects of human understanding and therefore the distinction between them depends solely on this understanding. Once this is appreciated, it becomes much easier to see that nature, like childhood, is not a fixed, immutable entity but a responsive concept, tied to our wider thinking, to our political and social concerns, to the meaning we want to make, and the kind of people we want to be (Lamb, 1996). What also becomes simultaneously clear is that if nature is a construct of human thought then any understanding of nature is liable to be a changeable, shifting phenomenon, open to making and remaking in varied and restless forms (Demeritt, 2002).

Why does the natural child matter?

If establishing the division between the natural and cultural is largely a matter of philosophical niceties and semantics, it might be reasonably asked as to why this matters to the study of childhood? Children will, after all, continue to be children in spite and not because of any such labelling. Yet despite the philosophical difficulties of establishing the concept of the natural child, it is a designation that does matter because, as I shall discuss below, there are powerful political incentives attached to the establishment of the natural. If childhood, or some aspect of it, can be held to be a natural phenomenon, this provides a foundation from which further understanding can be built. If childhood can be successfully grounded in such a solid base as that of nature, then considerable control has simultaneously been gained over what childhood should mean and how it should be enacted. Thus the contention here is that new, contemporary calls to natural childhood and natural children embody political desires and challenges to the dominant discourse of the 21st-century child.

In the next two sections I explore two understandings of the natural child and look at the philosophical basis of the understandings of 'natural' in each case.

The child as a natural object

Scientifically speaking, the term 'natural' refers to the elements of the physical universe (Barnes, 1974). These elements may exist without the presence of human beings (matter, energy, gravity) or they may exist because of human beings (bridges, robots, pollution). What binds them together in the heritage of post-enlightenment scientific enquiry is that such things behave in accordance with regular and discoverable laws. These laws form the basis of our scientific world-order. They transcend time and space and it is in their unchanging and universal character that the basis of the scientific enterprise lies. The timeless and fixed quality of these laws allows for the scientific method; it allows the world to be investigated in a logical fashion and holds forth the promise that an underlying order can be revealed. Experimentation, hypothesis building, testing and predicting are made possible through the belief in a rule-governed natural world. The character of the natural confirms its own positivist ontology: a concrete level of reality, which allows for the pursuit of certain knowledge (Barnes, 1974). The scientific enterprise regards the child as an object which can be investigated, like pollution, gravity or other natural phenomena, through the methods of science and understood according to scientific laws. Science is the study of the natural; the child as the object of scientific investigation fixes the child within its sphere; the natural child and the scientifically investigable child are one and the same.

Alan Prout (2008) traces the history of the child as the object of scientific investigation, pointing in particular to the development of two specific disciplines which have worked to examine, and therefore simultaneously to reify, the child as a natural object. These disciplines are paediatrics and developmental psychology. This latter has had particular implications for the trajectory of modern childhood studies. Most powerfully influenced by Piaget, although drawing on much earlier philosophical ideas, as Matthews and Mullin (2015) point out, this understanding of the child is grounded in the idea of cognitive development understood as a biologically-given process. The child matures through pre-given stages towards the stipulated outcome of adulthood. This does not imply that psychology has ignored the relevance of contextual factors in its investigations. Amongst many others, Judy Dunn and colleagues, for example, have conducted research which demonstrates the effects of family background on emotional understanding (Dunn et al., 1991) and Jim Stack (in Chapter 2) shows that when sharing tasks are framed within an everyday context children share at more equal levels and at younger ages than they would in windfall contexts. However, whilst these socially-embedded and evolutionary factors are important in informing our understanding of development in childhood, they rely exclusively on the scientific method and therefore still situate the child as an object of the natural world.

This postulation of the natural, scientifically investigable child has had widespread and profound implications for the understanding and treatment of childhood and its relationship to adulthood. Development of the child's mind occurs through natural processes (as we see in Chapter 6); the young child is therefore governed by the biology of this unfolding and is consequently more natural than cultural. This developmental paradigm, rooted in the idea of the child as scientific object, has become established as the chief frame of understanding through which the child is addressed. It is a formulation which, as Rogers and Rogers (1998) assert, has seeped into understandings of the emotional, social and behavioural lives of children as well as their cognitive development, confirming the positioning of the child in nature.

Adults, in contrast to children, have achieved biological maturity and are therefore no longer so tightly tied to the pre-given trajectory of nature. This state of relative freedom allows culture to become the dominant influence of their being. The cultured adult stands in contrast to the natural child, but not just in contrast. The hierarchy of the adult over the child is secured by the meta-physical ordering in which the cultural is given precedence over the natural (Frank, 2003). The cultured adult is the obvious superior to the natural child, the line of authority secured by the metaphorical dominance of culture over nature. Culture is the force by which nature can be tamed and understood; culture is that which has the power to act over nature (Ortner, 1974). Given this hierarchy, the natural child needs to be transformed by adults from 'mere organism to a cultured human, teaching it manners and the proper ways to behave in order to be a bonafide member of the culture' (Ortner, 1974:18).

Between them, the developmental paradigm and the cultural superiority of adults have turned the concept of the natural child into a powerful political platform from which the state of childhood can be directed. Psychology on the one hand offers a scientific understanding of children as naturally developing organisms, whilst on the other hand the culturally superior position of adults allows adults to assume a position from which they can control the lives of children. This positioning is apparent in myriad forms, but perhaps where these two forces dovetail most neatly is in the field of education where the task of the superior adult has become to enable and assist the smooth running of children's development towards the end goal of cultured adulthood.

CASE STUDY 8.1 EXPLORING THE APPLICATION TO PRACTICE

In societies like ours, government policies and legislation institutionalise childhood in multiple ways from compulsory education to designating how children should sit in cars (Gov.uk, 2016). However the impact of this narrative of childhood is spread, heightened and maintained by its distillation into professional authority and by widespread public use of the care and educational establishments which put such ideas into practice. In line with the understandings provided by 'developmental psychology and a positivistic and empirical analytic paradigm' (Dahlberg and Moss, 2005: vi), early childhood provision can be seen from a functional point of view as consisting of designated spaces like nurseries and schools in which children are exposed to programmes specifically designed to result in particular and pre-designated outcomes (Dahlberg and Moss, 2005: vi). Thus, this particular and powerful concept of the natural child, in both its scientific and metaphysical aspects, has led to a physical and social reality of childhood with very real consequences that determine the lives of children and their families.

The paradox however is, as Alan Prout argues, that the scientifically objectified natural child 'has helped to create an intellectual climate in which childhood was no longer seen to occur naturally. It did this by promoting the idea that childhood needed the attention and intervention of experts' (Prout, 2008: 25). So we have moved from the natural child whose development is governed by a pre-determined unfolding biology to a child whose development has to be carefully nurtured and managed by trained specialists. It is this paradox, I suggest, which has created the space for a new 21st-century notion of the natural child to emerge. Childhood, via ideas of biology and cultural status, has taken on a very particular form in our society. The space for dissent is clear; both history and ethnography tell us that this particular form is not inevitable, and both politics and social anthropology tell us that it cannot be defended against other forms of childhood as being somehow innately 'right'. What is perhaps unexpected though is that this space is being filled with a different version of the natural child. This version begins not with the idea of the child as an object but with the idea of the child as a subject whose 'naturalness' is an authenticity grounded in particular social practices rather than in scientific knowledge.

The child as a natural subject

Since the 1970s an alternative interpretation of the natural, with reference to children and childhood, has been undergoing construction. The genesis of this movement is frequently traced to Jean Liedloff's book *The Continuum Concept* (1975). Liedloff spent time living with the Ye'kuana Indians, an Amazonian people living in Venezuela, and through her subsequent publication urged western parents to adopt the childcare traditions she had observed there. These consisted in practices of close and continuous physical contact, including co-sleeping, constant carrying of immobile infants, immediate response to child cues including breastfeeding on demand, and recognition of the innate subjectivity of the child, from birth on, as a social and worthy being. Her argument rested on the idea that the human child, instinctively and evolutionarily, is designed for a particular lifestyle, as demonstrated by the Ye'kuana. For the human child, she argues, this is a way of life which 'has been natural to his kind for 99.9 percent of its history' (1975: 48) and to which the human infant is uniquely adapted. Emulating the Ye'kuana lifestyle therefore answers to young children's instinctive and evolutionarily designed desires and needs, and constitutes a natural way for children to be brought up.

Liedloff's ideas were taken up and widely spread by William Sears, an American parenting guru and prolific author of parenting literature (see for example Sears and Sears, 2001). Her principles are also discernible (and sometimes directly referenced) in the work of many other contemporary advocates of natural parenting and natural childhood. Similar ideas have also been explored in academic circles. Regine Schoen and Maarit Silven (2007) for example have researched what they describe as 'an age-old approach to parenting recently rediscovered in Western industrialized societies and known by names such as natural parenting, attachment parenting, and instinctive parenting' (Schoen and Silven, 2007: 102). Their subsequent analysis covers a range of practices such as breast feeding, attachment, co-sleeping and parental responsiveness to infant needs.

A proliferation of blogs, websites and on-line forums are testimony to the growing interest in these ideas (Freeman, 2016) and offer advice and discussion to a following that appears to have been on the increase for the past four decades. Key topics continue to circle around Liedloff's initial points of interest but have become combined with other issues, principally those of 'green' living. Frequently cited subjects include drug-free birth, home birth, long-term and demand breast feeding, baby wearing, attachment parenting, co-sleeping, home education, environmentally sustainable lifestyles, healthy eating, organic food and products, reusable nappies, recycling and free cycling, experiential learning and unschooling. These interests are often explicitly premised by the word 'natural', as in natural birth, natural parenting, natural learning, natural lifestyles.

This connection to the natural continues to be premised on the same grounds which Liedloff made in the 1970s. Peter Gray, an advocate of natural learning, for example asserts that human beings are naturally predisposed to a certain way of life which has accompanied humankind through its history and has only relatively recently been abandoned (Gray, 2013). The way of life which he cites is that of hunter-gatherers who for tens of thousands of years pursued, and in limited examples continue to pursue albeit in altered form, the 'original' existence of human beings. Like Liedloff, he argues for an evolutionary predisposition to this way of life: 'genetically we are all hunter–gatherers' (Gray, 2013: 22). His society of example is that of the Ju/hoansi of the Kalahari and he cites much the same arguments as Liedloff, although the Ye'kuana are not hunter–gatherers but settled cultivators and craftspeople (Olsen, 1991). Whilst quoting the genetic predisposition to this lifestyle, Gray's understanding of the childhoods of the Ju/hoansi is based more on cultural values than evolutionary adaptation. A non-schooled, play-rich childhood allows for cultural acquisition based on what he describes as 'children's natural, hunter–gatherer ways of learning' (Gray, 2013: 41). Strong traditional ideals of autonomy, sharing and equality, he argues, form a basis for trustful parenting which enables children to lead their own learning and to voluntarily make their own contributions to society. His endorsement of this way of life is made through its association with the natural. 'This' he argues, 'is childhood as nature designed it' (2013: 22). The thrust of the argument is that some childhoods are better than others, based on an appeal to the natural as being a condition or way of life that is fundamentally and more authentically human than other states or lifestyles.

This intertwining of value, authenticity and the natural is made through two deeply engrained cultural guises. In one of these nature is presented as the powerful constructor – the ultimate determiner of destiny. This is an argument with powerful contemporary resonance, running as it does through climate change debates and environmental protection arguments. Foolhardy human behaviour and a lack of respect for nature have resulted in a collision course which will lead to catastrophic outcomes for humanity. Nature's adaptability is pushed until inherent limits are reached – the 'tipping points' of radical climate change thinkers (Giddens, 2008). The forces of nature's retribution will then be released and 'a violent reminder of the power of nature and our own fragilities' (Giddens, 2008: 5) will be delivered. As the natural parenting movement is one which has become associated with green concerns it is an argument that slips over easily into thinking about natural childhoods.

Taking up this thread, Gray argues that we depart from nature's intention for children at our peril lest we are here too delivered of a natural retribution. Nature is presented as a personified force, endowed with intention which has designed the child to fit a particular cultural niche. The argument has scientific reference in the way it is proposed: that it is evolutionary adaptation and genetic makeups which pre-dispose humans towards certain ways of living. Yet it is the cultural response to these things which determine whether a childhood is natural or not. So, argues Gray, children have innate instincts to educate themselves through play and a natural childhood is one in which cultural arrangements accommodate this instinct. If the human response to nature's plan wanders into lifestyles too far from this niche however, then as in the climate change arguments thresholds will be reached. Thus, cautions Gray, in the modern, schooled west 'we are pushing the limits of children's adaptability' (Gray, 2013: 5). Schoen and Silven similarly argue with reference to their version of natural parenting that it 'is yet to be determined how much departure from this prototype of optimal human parenting is possible without compromising infant and parental well-being' (Schoen and Silven, 2007: 102). Hence we are warned of the consequences that will follow if certain boundaries of resilience and stability are crossed.

In its second strand, the argument presents nature as the weaker force, putting forward the view instead that humankind must take responsibility for its protection. If nature is not actively defended it will be lost through neglect or destruction, not just to the detriment of humanity but also ultimately to include the loss of humanity itself (Kompridis, 2009). Nature here is being invoked as an original, and therefore temporal, state of authenticity. The natural is to be found in history as a fundamental state or way of being, whether this is with reference to a given eco-system or to a human way of life. The history of our planet is a journey away from the original state with an accompanying loss of authenticity, so that as Gray laments, 'We have lost sight of the natural way to raise children' (2013: 19).

Thus this line of thinking promotes a call to arms to protect and defend natural childhood, to ensure its continuation.

CASE STUDY 8.2 EXPLORING THE APPLICATION TO PRACTICE

Here the authentic form of existence has been intertwined with an appeal to nature that owes its meaning not to science but to more everyday invocations of what is fundamentally right or good. This use of natural as the idea of wholesomeness, an expression of essential goodness, is a widespread one. It can be discerned in calls to protect environments: 'from this perspective nature must be defended against its "destruction" by humans and ... its "pristine" character' preserved (Castree and Braun, 1998: 4). But it is equally employable as a marketing device used in promoting all manner of products and practices, not least within the natural parenting community itself. Hence the natural is not only an original or intended state of being but also a good or morally right one. Yet as Baggini points out, this connection between the natural and the good and the unnatural and the bad is one based not on any form of logic: ' ... even if we agree that some things are natural and some are not, what follows from this? The answer is nothing' (Baggini, 2003: 181/2). Instead the association between the natural and the good rests on an evaluative premise of what constitutes good and bad rather than on rationality. The elasticity of the term 'natural' however stretches across meanings. So when Schoen and Silven (2007) write that 'considering all the evidence presented, natural parenting seems to provide the human infant with an ideal environment for optimal growth both psychologically and physiologically' (Schoen and Silven, 2007: 154), scientific facts and social values combine seamlessly into an argument for directing the lives of children in particular ways.

In this entanglement of meaning, nature emerges as a worthy moral guide for thinking about the lives of young children. A personified nature, inherently both authentic and good, acts as a righteous pilot pointing towards a particular childhood, with both the carrot that this is the ethical path to take and the stick that forces beyond human control may be unleashed if childhood is transgressed. The ground is thereby laid for a restoration of the natural child from object of scientific investigation to subject of particular social and educative practices.

From the Natural Child to the Political Child

Twenty-first century thought has turned questions of epistemology towards social constructionism. If we want to understand children, we must look to the context in which that understanding is built. In such a philosophy the positive ontology of the natural child seems doomed. Yet the natural child appears to be alive and kicking and to have lost none of its appeal.

There seem to be two reasons for this. Firstly that, as the above discussion hopes to have shown, the natural, like the child, is a subject open to endless reinvention.

Paradoxically, the natural child continues to exist precisely because social constructivism allows for the concept of the natural to be built and rebuilt in just the same way as the concept of the child can be. Meaning both seeps in and leeches out as the natural is recast in different places, at different times and for different purposes. So the invocation of the natural serves to connect rather than disconnect our understandings of childhood to actual spaces and times, creating a depth of meaning that the image of the natural child might at first seem intent on shedding. The natural child becomes part of a world view, a conduit for other concerns, aspirations, ideas, patterns of argument. It is this very contextualised nature of the natural that has allowed its reinvention in thinking about childhood.

Secondly, and begged by this first assertion, there continues to be considerable political mileage in establishing what is natural to children. Despite the postmodern turn of crumbling nature/culture boundaries (Prout, 2008), and the accompanying implications that could turn childhood into a non-linear, non-teleological space, the political arena of childhood remains heavily delineated (Dahlberg and Moss, 2005) and it is extraordinarily hard to envisage a future in which this would not be the case. Within this delineation the invocation of natural continues to be a powerful political tool. As both arguments regarding the natural presented above demonstrate, the natural is not just a designation but also a call to action, and it is this that makes the struggle over its meaning and who makes that meaning one of such importance. As Bruno Latour has put it, 'questions of epistemology are also questions of social order' (Demeritt (quoting Latour), 2002: 771). The establishment of what is natural to childhood carries with it immense power to shape the lives of children and their families. Colonising the natural in the political arguments of what childhood is and how it should be spent therefore remains important territory. As Valkanova argues, 'within early childhood education theory and practice, representations of nature ... have become sites of negotiation and struggle' (Valkanova, 2015: 17) and look set to continue to be so.

QUESTIONS FOR REFLECTION

1. In what other ways have ideas about nature and children been linked to each other?

2. Consider your own ideas about children and nature – on what grounds do you think you make those connections?

3. Must all ways of thinking about children entail the political?

SUMMARY

This chapter explores the notion of the natural child by looking at two different examples of how the natural has been used in understandings of childhood; the child as a natural object and the child as a natural subject. Through these examples it has been argued that the natural is a socially-constructed phenomenon which can be constructed and reconstructed in the light of new and changing ideas and concerns about nature as well as about children. For this reason, the natural child is a social construction in the same way that the child is a social construction. There is, therefore, no reason to think that changing ideas about childhood will make the concept of the natural child a redundant one. Rather, this chapter suggests that the natural child continues to have an important political salience.

End of chapter glossary

- **Epistemology** is a branch of philosophy that studies the theory of knowledge and the justification of belief.
- The **scientific construction of childhood** describes a knowledge of childhood, which is shaped by interpretations believed to be inherent to the state of childhood.
- The **scientific use of the term nature** refers to the phenomena of the physical universe that behave according to discoverable laws.
- **Social construction of childhood** describes a knowledge of childhood, which is shaped through interpretations of a wider context, for example politics, culture and philosophy.
- **Social constructivism** details that human development is socially situated.
- **Structuralist thinking** is based on the belief that all human culture and language can be understood in terms of common ordering principles typically represented by contrasting binary oppositions.

Further reading

Jenks, C. (2005) *Childhood*. Oxford: Routledge.
Taylor, A. (2013) *Reconfiguring the Natures of Childhood*. London: Routledge.

References

Baggini, J. (2003) *Making Sense: Philosophy Behind the Headlines*. Oxford: OUP.
Barnes, B. (1974) *Scientific Knowledge and Sociological Theory*. London: Routledge and Kegan Paul.
Bodnar, I. (2012) 'Aristotle's Natural Philosophy'. In E. Zalta (ed.), *The Stanford Encyclopedia of Philosophy*. Available at http://plato.stanford.edu/archives/spr2012/entries/aristotle-natphil/ (last accessed 29 March 2017).
Castree, N. and Braun, B. (1998) 'The Construction of Nature and theNature of Construction: Analytical and Political Tools for Building Survivable Futures'. In N. Castree and B. Braun (eds), *Remaking Reality: Nature at the Millennium*. London: Routledge.
Dahlberg, G. and Moss, P. (2005) *Ethics and Politics in Early Childhood Education*. Oxford: RoutledgeFalmer.
Demeritt, D. (2002) What is the 'social construction of nature'? A typology and sympathetic critique, *Progress in Human Geography*, 26 (6).
Descola, P. (2013) *Beyond Nature and Culture*. Chicago: Chicago University Press.

Dunn, J., Brown, J., Slomkowski, C., Tesla, C. and Youngblade, L. (1991) Young children's understanding of other people's feelings and beliefs: individual differences and their antecedents, *Child Development*, 62 (6).

Eagly, A. and Wood, W. (2013) The Nature-nurture debate: 25 years of challenges in understanding the psychology of gender, *Perspectives on Psychological Science*, 8 (3).

4Children (2015) What to expect, when? Guidance to your child's learning and development in the early years foundation stage. Available at www.4Children.org.uk (last accessed 29 March 2017).

Frank, R. (2003) Shifting identities: the metaphorics of nature-culture dualism in Western and Basque models of self, *metaphorik.de* 4. Available at www.metaphorik.de/04/frank. pdf (last accessed 28 March 2017).

Freeman, H. (30 July 2016) Attachment Parenting: The best way to raise a child – or maternal masochism. Available at www.theguardian.com/lifeandstyle/2016/jul/30/ attachment-parenting-best-way-raise-child-or-maternal-masochism (last accessed 29 March 2017).

Giddens, A. (2008) *The Politics of Climate Change*. London: Policy Network. Available at www.policy-network.net/uploadedFiles/Publications/Publications/The_politics_of_ climate_change_Anthony_Giddens.pdf (last accessed 29 March 2017).

Gray, P. (2013) *Free to Learn*. New York: Basic.

Gov.uk (2016) Child car seats: the law. Available at www.gov.uk/child-car-seats-the-rules/ when-a-child-can-travel-without-a-car-seat (last accessed 28 March 2017).

Jenks, C. (2005) *Childhood*. Oxford: Routledge.

Kompridis, N. (2009) Technology's challenge to democracy: What of the human?, *Parrhesia*, 8.

Lamb, K. (1996) The problem of defining nature first: a philosophical critique of environmental ethics, *Social Science Journal*, 33 (4).

Lancy, D (2015) *The Anthropology of Childhood*. Cambridge: Cambridge University Press.

Liedloff, J. (1975) *The Continuum Concept*. London: Penguin.

Matthews, G. and Mullin, A. (2015) 'The Philosophy of Childhood'. In E. Zalta (ed.), *The Stanford Encyclopedia of Philosophy*. Available at http://plato.stanford.edu/archives/ spr2015/entries/childhood/ (last accessed 29 March 2017).

Olsen, J. (1991) *The Indians of Central and South America: An Ethnohistorical Dictionary*. Westport, CT: Greenwood.

Ortner, S. (1974) 'Is Female to Male as Nature is to Culture?' In M.Z. Rosaldo and L. Lamphere (eds), *Woman, Culture, and Society*. Stanford, CA: Stanford University Press.

Prout, A. (2008) 'Culture-Nature and the Construction of Childhood'. In S. Livingstone and K. Drotner (eds), *The International Handbook of Children, Media and Culture*. London: Sage.

Rogers, R. and Rogers, W. (1998) 'Word Children'. In K. Leskni-Oberstein (ed.), *Children in Culture*. London: Macmillan.

Schoen, R. and Silven, M. (2007) Natural parenting – back to basics in infant care, *Evolutionary Psychology*, 5 (1).

Sears, W. and Sears, M. (2001) *The Attachment Parenting Book*. Massachusetts: Little, Brown and Company.

Taylor, A. (2013) *Reconfiguring the Natures of Childhood*. London: Routledge.

Valkanova, Y. (2015) 'Constructions of Nature and Emerging Ideas in Children's Education and Care, the 1600s to 1900'. In T. David, K. Goouch and S. Powell (eds), *The Routledge International Handbook of Philosophies and Theories of Early Childhood*. London: Routledge.

9
THE POOR CHILD

BABS ANDERSON AND ALEX OWEN

CHAPTER OBJECTIVES

- To examine the impact of poverty on children in the United Kingdom context.
- To consider diverse means to ameliorate this impact on children and their families.
- To locate poverty within a social justice framework.

Poverty is a troubling concept, affecting human societies across the globe. Simplistic definitions of poverty, such as lack of access to water, food and shelter, reflect Maslow's hierarchy of needs (1943) relating this to the deficiency of needs on the basis of physiological well-being and physical safety. A slightly more sophisticated approach includes the notion of relative poverty, where the individual or family is located within a socio-cultural context reflecting the norms and expectations of that society (Dex and Joshi, 2005). Yet another measure of poverty is child deprivation (UNICEF Innocenti Research Centre, 2012) where deprivation is considered as 'lacking two or more of 14 items considered normal and necessary for a child in an economically advanced country' (2012: 3). These latter two measures move away from the attainment of simple human requirements to sustain life to a more nuanced phenomenological understanding that life is experienced within a social context, that changes over time and place, and that it is relative to the life experiences of others within this shared space.

The United Kingdom context

In order to differentiate between these measures, the Department for Work and Pensions in the United Kingdom currently distinguishes between absolute low income and relative low income as a means of assessing poverty levels at the family income level. In the United Kingdom there were almost four million children living in poverty in the year 2015. This number has been shown to increase over recent times, with 0.5 million more British children living in absolute poverty in 2015 than in 2010 (DWP, 2015). Therefore, it appears that economic deprivation currently plays a significant role in over a quarter of all children's lives within the United Kingdom (Bunyan and Diamond, 2014). This has a range of effects upon the present-day experience and future life chances of the children involved. The inequality of experience is revealed in the holistic development of a child living within the context of poverty as early as 22 months of age (Whitham, 2012). This disparity, experienced from the very beginning of life, may then proliferate through each stage of childhood, resulting in a significant impact on a child's future life chances (Field, 2010; Odgers et al., 2012). Child poverty can impact on a child's grades in school (DfE, 2015) and therefore the child's educational outcomes. It can affect a child's diet (Miller and Korenman, 1994), such as access to nutrient-rich foodstuffs, a child's general health, such as exposure to air-borne pollutants in the local environment, and a child's life expectancy (ONS, 2014), thus indicating poorer health outcomes over the lifespan. It may also impact on a child's resourcefulness (Hanson et al., 1997), a child's likelihood to suffer a mental illness (Dornfeld and Kruttschnitt, 1992), a child's social-emotional development (Keegan, 2001), and a child's friendship relationships (Patterson et al., 1991). Hence the child's socio-emotional and personal outcomes may be compromised due to the experience of growing up in poverty. The experience of childhood for children living in poverty shows significant differences from that of their more affluent peers (Wilkinson and Pickett, 2010).

It is estimated that child poverty costs British society £29 billion per year (Hirsch, 2008) and it is clear that a major driver in the desire to address this is primarily that of economics rather than social justice. In an attempt to address this issue, the Labour government of the early 21st century pledged to eradicate child poverty by the year 2020. The Child Poverty Act of 2010 detailed the legislation which evolved in response to this political assurance, and although there has been a change in political power since this pledge, all political parties have continued to articulate their support of the agenda, at least in rhetoric (DWP and DfE, 2011; DWP and DfE, 2012).

Factors in child poverty

There is a range of factors, associated with the structure of a family, that can increase the likelihood that a child will develop within a context of economic deprivation. These include if the family involves a single parent, if the family is from a non-White British background, if the family does not own the house that they live in or if the mother left school without post-16 qualifications (Bradshaw and Holmes, 2010). Yet the family is where a child spends much of their formative years and therefore the quality of the familial environment is of crucial importance (Tickell, 2011). The parent/child relationship has been shown to be fundamental to the development of a child (Siraj-Blatchford and Siraj-Blatchford, 2009). However, poverty can have a significant impact upon the atmosphere in the family context, involving the home learning environment, parental nurturing, parental mental well-being, child resilience and school readiness, resulting in the child's present-day life experience and future life chances being consistently undermined (Dex and Joshi, 2005; Hansen et al., 2010).

These negative implications of child poverty may be due to the stress felt on a daily basis within the family context. The familial environment, within a context of economic deprivation, is often infused with an atmosphere of low-level anxiety regarding the financial position of the family (Pearlin, 1989). There have been links made between this daily strain and parental depression resulting in an impact upon the parent/child relationship. Parental depression reduces a parent's coping capacity, thus inhibiting their ability to show warmth, to nurture and to care for a child (Evans and English, 2003; Wandsworth et al., 2008). Additionally, depression can reduce the parent's own personal resilience, and hence leading to a negative effect upon their mental well-being, social engagement and proactive accessing of external support interventions (Pearlin et al., 1981; Petterson and Burke Albers, 2003). All parents can engage in unhelpful child-directed behaviours, yet the pressure exerted on the family within a context of poverty has been shown to have the potential to increase the stress felt by the parents involved (Wilson, 1991; Barnes and Freude-Lagevardi, 2002).

Obviously, not all children respond in the same way. A child's personality, within a context of poverty, can moderate some of the negative effects of parental child-directed behaviours (McLoyd, 1990). Additionally, not all parents living within a context of poverty are affected in the same negative manner. Not all economically disadvantaged parents suffer from depression as a result of the worry felt concerning the financial security of their family. Also, not all parents who suffer from depression engage in unsupportive child-directed behaviours (Klebanov et al., 1994; Jackson, 2000). Research reveals that if a family adapts their lifestyle to the pressures of an economically deprived environment, then the stress experienced can be negated to such a degree that the child's development is supported (Elder and Caspi, 1988). This said, the value of supportive parenting is clear and practice has sought to respond to the needs of parents accordingly.

Support for families in poverty

External support is one of the key resources available to parents within this context (Kirk, 2003; Attree, 2004). External support falls within two broad categories – formal support interventions and informal social support mechanisms. The objective of formal support interventions, for instance parenting classes, is usually to educate parents about appropriate parenting behaviours, thus developing attitudes and skills that seek to negate the effects of poverty (Edwards and Gillies, 2004). These interventions are effective in some contexts and have been shown to decrease incidences of child neglect in some deprived environments (Edwards et al., 2007; Whittaker and Cowley, 2012).

Yet for some parents, these formal mechanisms of support are regarded with a high level of distrust and are therefore avoided (Heinrichs et al., 2005; Peters et al., 2005). In particular, single-parent mothers, residing within a low socio-economic context, have been shown to be most wary of the social welfare agencies and health professionals who deliver a significant proportion of the formal support interventions on offer (McKendrick et al., 2003; Attree, 2004).

Informal support networks

As an alternative to these formal support interventions, informal social support networks also have significance in supporting the parents of young children (Broadhead et al., 1983; Bloom, 1990). The outcome of informal social support interventions, for instance the friendships built between parents on the 'school run', is usually to support parents socio-emotionally, developing parental resilience and ability to cope with the aim to negate the effects of poverty (Ghate and Hazel, 2002; Edwards and Gillies, 2004). This form of support network supports parents at an emotional level, so that by providing a friendly interest in the concerns of the parent, their feelings of insignificance and lack of competence are therefore reduced. Also, this form of support assists parents at an informative level, providing direction that moderates feelings of perplexity and the inability to deal authoritatively with the demands of parenting. Finally, this support provides encouragement at an instrumental level, providing physical assistance to oppose the feelings of being unable to control the events that take place (Cohen, 2004). In opposition to a commonly-held misconception that poor environments are usually socially fragmented, it has been found that the majority of parents living in economically-deprived environments have three or more adults from whom they can achieve informal social support (Ghate and Hazel, 2002; Attree, 2004). These social support relationships, usually with either friends or family, act as a protective factor for a child against the influences of poverty (Cochran et al., 1990). The defence created by these relationships operates at an initial and ancillary level. The initial defence is a result of the supportive relationships that can be built between a grandmother, for example, who is part of the parent's informal support network, and the child directly. This protective factor can have a profound effect in terms of the support of a child's development by countering negative parental behaviours that may be experienced, acting as an illustration of alternative forms of adult behaviour. The ancillary defence is a result of the supportive relationships that can be built between an adult friend, for example, and the parent. This protective factor can have a helpful effect in terms of a parent's child-directed behaviours as the parent is challenged to moderate their behaviour through the child-directed behaviours they witness demonstrated by their friends, for instance (Cochran et al., 1990). Parents encounter alternative models of parenting by observing them in action, and in doing so may emulate these whether consciously or not (Owen and Anderson, 2015). In this way, an example of this is where the parent's repertoire of coping behaviours can be more positive when dealing with the demands of young children's behaviour.

Formal support structures

As discussed above, some formal structures are targeted at specific groups, such as parenting support programmes (Edwards and Gillies, 2004) offered by a range of services including Sure Start Children's Centres, health clinics, or charitable organisations such as Barnardo's. Others aim to improve the life chances of children through a range of interventions based in school settings and early education and care (ECEC) settings. These include the 'Two-year old offer', an extension of the free entitlement for all 3 to 4 year-olds in England for 570 hours of free early education or childcare per year (HMG, 2016). The extension to 2 year-olds is a targeted intervention, where the specific criteria used to determine eligibility correspond to deprivation indices. In this way, the government seeks to improve children's life chances by supporting their learning and development from outside the familial home environment. How successful this will be in reducing the attainment gap in 22-month-old children, identified by Whitham (2012) above, remains to be seen.

The Pupil Premium (HMG, 2016) also delivers a set amount of funding as available to support the development of children who meet certain criteria indicating need. Deemed successful in supporting schools' attempts to reduce the achievement gap between children, the philosophy underpinning the Pupil Premium was extended in 2014 to encompass the Early Years Pupil Premium, whereby Early Childhood Education and Care (ECEC) settings were enabled to access sources of additional funding (ibid). The case study below shows a model letter for all ECEC settings to send to parents to ascertain how many of the children attending their setting are eligible for this type of additional funding. A form is also sent to parents with this letter to collect some of the data required to assess entitlement.

CASE STUDY 9.1   EXPLORING COMMUNICATION WITH PARENTS

The following is a model letter for early years settings to send to all parents to inform them of the Early Years Pupil Premium.

Dear Parent,

The Early Years Pupil Premium

From April 2015, nurseries, schools, childminders and other childcare providers have been able to claim extra funding through the Early Years Pupil Premium to support children's development, learning and care. We wanted to write to you to explain what the Early Years Pupil Premium is, explain who is eligible for this funding and, importantly, to ask you to fill out the enclosed forms so that we as a provider can claim the extra funding.

National data and research tells us that children eligible for free school meals tend to do less well, for example in 2014, 45% of children eligible for free school meals achieved the expected level at the end of the early years foundation stage

(Continued)

(Continued)

compared with 64% of other children. The Early Years Pupil Premium will provide us with extra funding to close this gap.

The Early Years Pupil Premium provides an extra 53 pence per hour for three and four year old children whose parents are in receipt of certain benefits or who were formerly in local authority care but who left care because they were adopted or were subject to a special guardianship or child arrangements order. This means an extra £302 a year for each child taking up the full 570 hours funded entitlement to early education. This additional money could make a significant difference to us.

We can use the extra funding in any way we choose to improve the quality of the early years education that we provide for your child. This could include, for example, additional training for our staff on early language, investing in partnership working with our colleagues in the area to further our expertise or supporting our staff in working on specialised areas such as speech and language.

It is well documented that high quality early education can influence how well a child does at both primary and secondary school so we do want to make the most of this additional funding. You may be aware if you have older children that a pupil premium has been available for school-age children and it has proved to have given a real boost to the children receiving the funding. We want to do the same for our early years children entitled to this funding.

Therefore we ask that ALL PARENTS/GUARDIANS fill in the attached form. This will allow us to claim the additional Early Years Pupil Premium.

If you have any questions, please contact *[add contact details here]*.

Source: https://www.gov.uk/government/publications/early-years-pupil-premium-model-document-and-letter-for-parents (last accessed 28.9.16)

The letter above illustrates the possible positive effect of pupil premium funding in schools and relates this to the quality of the setting. The letter presents to parents the idea that the Early Years Pupil Premium will be used to boost the quality of the ECEC setting. This matches the rhetoric of educational policy (Ball, 2008) that suggests a failure to close the 'gap' for children in poverty and their more affluent peers lies within the gift of educational practitioners rather than acknowledging broader more wide-ranging societal issues. The effects of austerity measures, in terms of reducing the availability of formal parenting support mechanisms, such as those offered by Sure Start Children's Centres (Sammons et al., 2015), have also moved the onus away from family support to targeted support for individual children in educational institutions, such as schools and ECEC settings. Thus the direction of support lies at an institutional level, which can then be held accountable for results rather than viewing poverty as a social justice issue of inclusion, with responsibility held by the whole of society (Bennett et al., 2016).

A wider perspective

The (2010) Marmot report on 'Fair Society, Healthy Lives' gives six policy objectives, proposing that social inequality results in a 'social gradient of health' (2010: 9). Social position directly influences health outcomes, whereby the lower the social position, the less favourable the health outcomes are. The recommendations are to:

- give every child the best start in life;
- enable all children to maximise their capabilities and have control over their lives;
- create fair employment and good work for all;
- ensure a healthy standard of living for all;
- create and develop healthy and sustainable places and communities;
- strengthen the role and impact of ill health prevention.

These six recommendations echo those of the Black report in 1980 (Pickett and Dorling, 2010), hence giving rise to the idea that the same concerns are present today, despite the passage of almost forty years. The need for more radical demands to create a more socially just landscape, such as implementing higher taxation levels on the more affluent, is not however readily apparent in the later document (ibid).

Of these six policy objectives above, the first is deemed the most important, that of giving every child the best start in life. This policy objective has three components (Marmot, 2010: 16), namely:

1 Reduce inequalities in the early development of physical and emotional health and cognitive, linguistic, and social skills.
2 Ensure high-quality maternity services, parenting programmes, childcare and early years education to meet needs across the social gradient.
3 Build the resilience and well-being of young children across the social gradient.

CASE STUDY 9.2   EXPLORING THE MARMOT INDICATORS

The Marmot indicators, as developed from these recommendations by the Institute of Health Equity (2015), have been used to analyse the success of local authorities in responding to these recommendations. One of the indicators in particular links to the pivotal nature of early childhood experiences with the recommendation of giving 'every child the best start in life'.

This document examines:

.... the comparative 'gap' between all pupils and those eligible for free school meals achieving a good level of development at age 5, both across years and regions. In England the 'gap' increased from 15.5 percentage points in 2012/13 to 15.6 percentage points in 2013/14. At a regional level, the gap increased in two-thirds of regions. In 2013/14, London

(Continued)

(Continued)

recorded the narrowest gap (9.9 percentage points), almost half that seen in the South West (18.9). In 2012/13, the 'school readiness' gap ranged from 9.8% in London to 18.8% in the South West.

At local authority level:

There is substantial variation in results across the country – at a local authority level, the 'gap' between all and FSM pupils in 2013/14 varied from a relatively narrow 4.2 percentage point 'gap' in Hackney, where 64.9% of all pupils and 60.7% of those eligible for free school meals achieved 5+ GCSEs or equivalent, to a relatively large 29.5 percentage point gap in Bath and North East Somerset, where 62.5% of all pupils and only 33% of those eligible for free school meals achieved 5+ GCSEs or equivalent. These variations suggest that there is more that can and should be done to reduce in-area inequalities.

Source: http://www.instituteofhealthequity.org/Content/FileManager/Indicators 2015/marmot-indicators-2015-background-document-final-26-11-15.pdf (last accessed 26.9.16).

The picture is one of a complex diversity of localised responses to a national issue. It indicates that some local authorities are making headway in their aim of reducing the 'gap' of attainment between those children receiving free school meals as a measure of deprivation and the average attainments of children across all social positions. It may be that certain Local Authorities have prioritised educational access and achieved success through this.

Yet the reasons for the differences may be wide ranging, with little heed taken of the differences within each geographical local authority location. For example, a rural local authority may have a different set of contextual characteristics that could impact on these scores, such as the challenges of rural poverty and lack of transport access to sources of support. The disintegration of traditional labour markets, requiring mobility of the workforce, and the number of agricultural migrant families with fewer available social support networks (as newcomers to the United Kingdom) are also issues, which may make complex demands on educational provision, for example. Simplifying such complex issues in this manner may be counter-productive in its laudable aims of improving social equity on a national basis.

The (2010) Marmot report sets out how a fair and equitable nation should proceed in response to reducing the level and significance of poverty in the United Kingdom. Yet this requires political and popular will, rather than just policy rhetoric, for it to succeed. Poverty and deprivation are significant factors in the lives of an increasing population of young children and their families. There are a range of support mechanisms that can moderate this, including formal and informal support networks, although it currently appears the major key to reducing child poverty is viewed as educational intervention by government rather than the nurturing of support networks.

QUESTIONS FOR REFLECTION

1. How might formal support structures for parents operate in practice?

2. Why would wearing a uniform by the early years' practitioners, such as a polo shirt with a logo, actually act as a barrier to the intended support? What cultural aspects might come into play here?

3. Why might informal support systems, such as friends and family, be seen as more non-judgemental for parents?

4. Are educational institutions an effective source of reducing the attainment 'gap' between children living in poverty and their more affluent peers?

5. What other mechanisms might support enhancement of educational, health and personal/socio-emotional outcomes for young children and their families? How accessible are these for children and their families living in rural areas or from other cultural groups?

SUMMARY

In this chapter we have considered what poverty is and the implications for a wide range of aspects of the young child's life, including educational, health and socio-emotional outcomes. There are two types of external support for young children and their families in terms of lessening the negative impact of poverty, which include formal interventions such as parenting programmes and the targeted Early Years Pupil Premium funding, in addition to informal support networks. The Marmot report (2010) gives a set of policy objectives in relation to the support of children living in poverty, but the application of these to reducing the impact of poverty remains inconsistent across the diversity of local authority contexts.

End of chapter glossary

*   **Child poverty** refers to the situation of a child living in a situation that fails to meet the acceptable standard of living for a particular society.
*   **Deprivation** describes when an individual lacks items that are considered normal and necessary for life in a particular social context.
*   **Formal support interventions** involve the formal mechanisms of support on offer to parents, for example parenting classes.
*   **Informal social support** refers to the informal relationships that result in providing an individual with socio-emotional support.
*   **Social justice** involves the promotion of fairness in relation to the distribution of wealth and opportunity within a society.

Further reading

Brown, Z. (ed.) (2016) *Inclusive Education: Perspectives on Pedagogy, Policy and Practice*. Abingdon: Routledge.
Marmot, M. (2015) *The Health Gap: The Challenge of an Unequal World*. London: Bloomsbury.

References

Attree, P. (2004) Parenting support in the context of poverty: a meta-synthesis of the qualitative evidence, *Journal of Health and Social Care in the Community*, 13 (4): 330–337.
Ball, S. (2008) *The Education Debate*. Bristol: Policy Press.
Barnes, J. and Freude-Lagevardi, A. (2002) *From Early Pregnancy to Early Childhood: Early Interventions to Enhance the Mental Health of Children and Families*. London: Mental Health Foundation.
Bennett, K., Mander, S. and Richards, L. (2016) 'Inclusive Practice for Families'. In Z. Brown (ed.), *Inclusive Education: Perspectives on Pedagogy, Policy and Practice*. Abingdon: Routledge.
Bloom, J. (1990) The relationship of social support and health, *Social Science and Medicine*, 30: 635–637.
Bradshaw, J. and Holmes, J. (2010) 'Child Poverty in the First Five Years of Life'. In K. Hansen, H. Joshi and S. Dex (eds), *Children of the 21st Century: The First Five Years*. Bristol: Policy.
Broadhead, W., Kaplan, B., James, S., Wagner, E., Schoenbach, R., Grimson, R., Heyden, S., Tibblin, G. and Gehlbach, S. (1983) The epidemiological evidence for a relationship between social support and health, *American Journal of Epidemiology*, 117 (5): 521–537.
Bunyan, P. and Diamond, J. (2014) *Approaches to Reducing Poverty and Inequality in the UK: A Study of Civil Society Initiatives and Fairness Commissions*. (A report commissioned by the Webb Memorial Trust for the All Party Parliamentary Group on Poverty.)
Cochran, M., Larner, M., Riley, D., Gunnarson, L. and Henderson, C. (1990) *Extending Families: The Social Networks of Parents and Their Children*. Cambridge: Cambridge University Press.
Cohen, S. (2004) Social relationships and health, *American Psychologist*, 59 (8): 676–684.
Department for Education (DfE) (2015) *Statistical First Release: GCSE and Equivalent Attainment by Pupil Characteristics 2013–2014*. London: Crown.
Department for Work and Pensions (DWP) (2015) *Households Below Average Income*. London: Crown.
Department for Work and Pensions (DWP) & Department for Education (DfE) (2011) *A New Approach to Child Poverty: Tackling the Causes of Disadvantage and Transforming Lives*. London: Crown.
Department for Work and Pensions (DWP) & Department for Education (DfE) (2012) *Child Poverty in the UK: The Report on the 2010 Target*. London: Crown.
Dex, S. and Joshi, H. (2005) *Children of the 21st Century: From Birth to 9 Months*. Bristol: Policy.
Dornfeld, M. and Kruttschnitt, C. (1992) Do the stereotypes fit? Mapping gender-specific outcomes and risk factors, *Criminology*, 30 (3): 397–419.
Edwards, R., Ceilleachair, A., Bywater, T., Hughes, D. and Hutchings, J. (2007) Parenting programmes for parents of children at risk of developing conduct disorder: cost effectiveness analysis, *British Medical Journal*, 334: 682.
Edwards, R. and Gillies, V. (2004) Support in parenting: values and consensus concerning who to turn to, *Journal of Social Policy*, 33 (4): 627–647.

Elder, G. and Caspi, A. (1988) Economic stress in lives: developmental perspectives, *Journal of Social Issues*, 44 (4): 25–45.

Evans, G. and English, K. (2003) The environment of poverty: multiple stressor exposure, psychophysiological stress, and socioemotional adjustment, *Child Development*, 73 (4): 1238–1248.

Field, F. (2010) *The Foundation Years: Preventing Poor Children Becoming Poor Adults.* The Report of the Independent Review on Poverty and Life Chances. London: Crown.

Ghate, D. and Hazel, N. (2002) *Parenting in Poor Environments: Stress and Coping.* London: Jessica Kingsley.

Hansen, K., Joshi, H. and Dex, S. (2010) *Children of the 21st Century: The First Five Years.* Bristol: Policy.

Hanson, T., McLanahan, S. and Thomson, E. (1997) 'Economic Resources, Parental Practices, and Children's Well-being'. In G. Duncan and J. Brooks-Gunn (eds), *Consequences of Growing Up Poor.* New York: Russell Sage Foundation.

Heinrichs, N., Bertram, H., Kuschel, A. and Hahlweg, K. (2005) Parent recruitment and retention in a universal prevention program for child behaviour and emotional problems: barriers to research and program participation, *Prevention Science*, 6: 275–286.

Her Majesty's Government (HMG) (2016) *Free Childcare and Education for 2-4 Year-Olds.* London: HMG. Available at www.gov.uk/help-with-childcare-costs/free-childcare-and-education-for-2-to-4-year-olds (last accessed 28 March 2017).

Hirsch, D. (2008) *Estimating the Cost of Child Poverty.* York: Joseph Rowntree Foundation.

Jackson, A. (2000) Maternal self-efficacy and children's influence on stress and parenting among single black mothers in poverty, *Journal of Family Issues*, 21 (1): 3–16.

Keegan, M. (2001) The effects of poverty on children's socioemotional development: an ecological systems analysis, *Social Work*, 46 (3): 256–266.

Kirk, R. (2003) Family support: the role of the Early Years' Centres, *Children and Society*, 17: 85–99.

Klebanov, P., Brooks-Gunn, J. and Duncan, G. (1994) Does neighborhood and family poverty affect mothers' parenting, mental health, and social support?, *Journal of Marriage and Family*, 56 (2): 441–455.

Marmot, M. (2010) *Fair Society, Healthy Lives: Strategic Review of Health Inequalities in England post-2010.* London: The Marmot Review

Maslow, A.H. (1943) A theory of human motivation, *Psychological Review*, 50 (4): 430–437

McKendrick, J., Cunningham-Burley, S. and Backett-Milburn, K. (2003) *Life in Low Income Families in Scotland.* Edinburgh: Scottish Executive.

McLoyd, V. (1990) The impact of economic hardship on black families and children: psychological distress, parenting and socioemotional development, *Child Development*, 61: 311–346.

Miller, J. and Korenman, S. (1994) Poverty and children's nutritional status in the United States, *American Journal of Epidemiology*, 140: 233–243.

Odgers, C., Caspi, A., Russell, M., Sampson, R., Arsenault, L and Moffirr, T. (2012) Supportive parenting mediates neighborhood socioeconomic disparities in children's antisocial behavior from ages 5 to 12, *Development and Psychopathology*, 24: 705–721.

Office for National Statistics (ONS) (2014) *Inequality in Healthy Life Expectancy at Birth by National Deciles of Area Deprivation: England, 2009–11.* London: Crown.

Owen, A. and Anderson, B. (2015) Informal community support for parents of pre-school children: a comparative study investigating the subjective experience of parents attending community-based toddler groups in different socio-economic situations, *Journal of Early Childhood Research online*:1–13. doi:10.1177/1476718X15597022.

Patterson, C., Vaden, N. and Kupersmidt, J. (1991) Family background, recent life events and peer rejection during childhood, *Journal of Social and Personal Relationships*, 8: 347–361.

Pearlin, L. (1989) The sociological study of stress, *Journal of Health and Social Behaviour*, 30: 241–256.

Pearlin, L., Lieberman, M., Menaghan, E. and Mullan, J. (1981) The stress process, *Journal of Health and Social Behaviour*, 22: 337–356.

Peters, S., Calam, R. and Harrington, R. (2005) Maternal attributions and expressed emotion as predictors of attendance at parent management training, *Journal of Child Psychology and Psychiatry*, 47: 99–111.

Petterson, S. and Burke Albers, A. (2003) Effects of poverty and maternal depression on early child development, *Child Development*, 72 (6): 1794–1813.

Pickett, K.E. and Dorling, D. (2010) Against the organization of misery? The Marmot Review of health inequalities, *Social Science and Medicine*, 71: 1231–1233.

Sammons, P., Hall, J., Smees, R. and Goff, J. (2015) DfE-RR495 'The impact of children's centres: studying the effects of children's centres in promoting better outcomes for young children and their families'. Evaluation of Children's Centres in England (ECCE, Strand 4). London: DfE.

Siraj-Blatchford, I. and Siraj-Blatchford, J. (2009) *Improving Children's Attainment through a Better Quality of Family-based Support for Early Learning*. London: Centre for Excellence and Outcomes in Children's and Young People's Services.

Tickell, C. (2011) *The Early Years: Foundations for Life, Health and Learning*. (An Independent Report on the Early Years Foundation Stage to Her Majesty's Government.) London: Crown.

UNICEF Innocenti Research Centre (2012) *Measuring Child Poverty: New League Tables of Child Poverty in the World's Rich Countries*, Innocenti Report Card 10. UNICEF: Innocenti Research Centre, Florence.

Wandsworth, M., Tali, R., Reinhard, C., Wolf, B., Decarlo Santiago, C. and Einhorn, L. (2008) An indirect effects model of the association between poverty and child functioning: the role of children's poverty-related stress, *Journal of Loss and Trauma: International Perspectives on Stress and Coping*, 13 (2–3): 156–185.

Whitham, G. (2012) *Child Poverty in 2012: It Shouldn't Happen Here*. London: Save the Children.

Whittaker, K. and Cowley, S. (2012) An effective programme is not enough: a review of factors associated with poor attendance and engagement with parenting programmes, *Children and Society*, 26: 138–149.

Wilkinson, R. and Pickett, K. (2010) *The Spirit Level: Why Equality is Better for Everyone*. London: Penguin.

Wilson, W. (1991) Studying inner city social dislocations: the challenge of public agenda research, *American Sociological Review*, 56 (1): 1–14.

10

THE FAT CHILD

LAURA WAITE AND ERIN PRITCHARD

CHAPTER OBJECTIVES

- Understand that body size is historically, socially and culturally constructed.
- Recognise that fatness and health are not necessarily synonymous.
- Appreciate that tackling fat stigma and fat prejudice is an important endeavour in improving children's health.

There is now considered to be a global 'obesity epidemic' which, so it is said, includes the problem of an ever-increasing number of fat children. *In this chapter the term fat is used, as opposed to obese or overweight, in order to discuss the fat child. Fat is the accepted term used by fat rights activists and our reason for employing this term will be discussed in more detail throughout the chapter.* According to the World Health Organisation (WHO, 2016) it is estimated that there are now over 170 million 'obese' children in the world. Furthermore, they suggest that 'childhood obesity' is one of the most serious public health challenges of the 21st century (WHO, 2016), with a fear that fat children turn into fat adults and that this leads to numerous health problems.

Despite the fact that there are many different causes of fatness, it is typically presented as only being caused by overeating and something that is the individual's fault, or as is often the case for children, the parent's fault. The dominant model of 'obesity', which has its roots in medicine, deems fatness to be a sign of greed, laziness, repulsiveness and something that needs to be prevented or cured (Cooper, 2016). Latner and Stunkard (2003) point out that the stigmatisation of the fat child has increased significantly since the 1960s, which can have all sorts of implications for fat children, such as bullying, invasive weight loss treatments, and in extreme cases, children being taken into care due to parent blame.

Focusing on children, this chapter aims to illuminate how a number of complex forces interact to create 'The Fat Child' and that any solution to helping children lead healthier lifestyles must take account of this complexity. Furthermore, we argue that there must be a recognition of the impact that fat stigma has on children and families and again that any improvement in the well-being of children cannot be achieved without addressing fat prejudice.

The 'O' word

'Obesity' is the accepted term to refer to fatness within the scientific literature, as well as within the British media. Cooper (1998) finds this term troublesome; it derives from the Latin *obedere* – *ob* meaning 'over' + *edere* from 'eat' (*OED*, 2004). This directly conjoins fatness with eating as opposed to other factors, such as genetics, medical conditions and side effects from medication. In addition, it ignores possible social and environmental causes and thus produces the common misconception that *the* cause of fatness is overeating. This misconception is further reinforced in the media through the iconic image of the fat child eating something deemed unhealthy (Herndon, 2014). Immediately a connection is made between a child's body size and their eating habits.

In relation to fat activism and fat studies, the word 'fat' is the accepted term, as opposed to others such as 'large', 'overweight' or 'obese'. Cooper (1998) explains that using the word 'fat' is about reclaiming the word and giving it a more positive and descriptive meaning. It does not imply that overeating is a cause of fatness, and thus refrains from blaming the individual for their size; fat can instead be perceived as a bodily difference. Rothblum (2012) extends this argument by suggesting that this act is in keeping with other oppressed groups who purposefully replace terms that would previously have been a medical or clinical diagnosis, for example 'homosexual'.

The 'obesity epidemic'

The rise in the number of fat people, including fat children, is often described as an 'obesity epidemic'. This term is commonly associated with disease, something that is spread from person to person, which carries all sorts of health problems including those that can potentially be fatal. Repeated use of the term 'obesity epidemic', especially in the news, encourages the assumption that there is a spreading phenomenon of overeating that is causing fatness and related health problems. However, as Gard and Wright (2005) point out, fatness is neither a disease nor an epidemic; using this term merely helps to incite panic into society and further stigmatises fat people. Cooper defines use of the term 'obesity epidemic' as 'a rhetorical device to leverage fat panic' (2016: 3). An epidemic is something considered as being out of control and in need of eradication in order to benefit society and the medical, diet and fitness industries are seen primarily as the solution to this eradication. Monaghan et al. (2013) argue that medical industries, such as the pharmaceutical industry, have a vested interest in the assertion that fatness is 'bad' and this can be seen in the increased use of prescription drug treatments for fat children (O'Dea, 2006) and weight-loss surgery. By promoting fatness as bad and something that should be eliminated, the pharmaceutical, diet and fitness industries have the potential to increase their business and make considerable profits. As O'Dea (2006) argues, it should be of serious concern that childhood obesity is being influenced by those who aim to make a profit from treatments, especially given that any weight loss achieved does not guarantee the various health benefits that many companies claim. As Rich and Evans (2005) argue, the data associated with the benefits of weight loss are often fragmented and ambiguous.

BMI

The WHO, as well as medical practitioners and researchers, continue to use the BMI as an indicator of obesity despite its limits being well documented (see for example Burkhauser and Cawley, 2008; Rothman, 2008). Furthermore, the BMI is considered to be a poor tool particularly for gauging fatness in children (Rich and Evans, 2005). As a measurement, it cannot distinguish body composition and thus fails to take into account an individual's muscle mass or bone structure. It is there-fore possible for an athlete, for example, to technically be classed as obese despite having very little fat tissue (Oliver, 2006).

Using the BMI, obesity goes from being a few pounds overweight to being morbidly obese. Whilst Rich and Evans (2005) acknowledge that the latter may have some associated health risks (although evidence that supports this claim will be taken up later in the chapter), health risks to the former are often over exag-gerated and contribute to the idea that the UK is suffering from an epidemic of national proportions.

A further problem with using the BMI is that it reveals nothing about an indi-vidual's health. As Rich and Evans (2005) argue, there are fat people who lead active and healthy lifestyles and thin people whose lifestyles would be deemed unhealthy and sedentary. It is therefore an erroneous belief that fatness and poor health go hand in hand despite the media's desire to have us believe otherwise.

Cultural representations of fat bodies

It has long been recognised that the media not only report on social issues but play an important role in their construction and fatness is no exception. It seems virtually impossible nowadays to turn on the television or open a newspaper without the so-called 'obesity epidemic' being discussed; indeed, Boero suggests that 'obesity' has become a 'mainstay of media' (2013: 371). This hyper-coverage, which is often alarmist in tone, usually includes humiliating images of fat bodies and typically features large expanses of stomach or backside in ill-fitting, casual clothing. These carefully selected images generally signify 'working class bodies' and serve to reinforce other discourses – 'the socially and economically unpro-ductive body', 'the out of control body'. The images are rarely of people dressed like professionals. They do not signify productivity and achievement; instead 'fat bodies are represented as inferior, deficient and ugly' (Lupton, 2014: 33). In addition to news coverage or magazine stories, there is also now a plethora of so-called 'reality shows' that feature fat people. These characteristically contain a fat person going on a harsh diet and exercise regime for 12 months with an 'expert' life-coach/personal trainer working alongside them, or fat children attending some sort of gruelling boot camp.

Dominant framing

Boero argues that the media typically frames fatness as either:

a)   medical – something that is genetic or disease-like;
b)   environmental – caused by fast food and inactivity; or
c)   individual/moral – caused by personal behaviour (2013: 373).

She contends, however, that the most dominant framing of the fat body is 'individual', which is not surprising given the current socio-political ideology which values self-control and self-determination. Boero (2013) however does draw attention to the contradictions at play in these representations. Firstly, the medical, environmental and moral framings would suggest that the causes of fatness are likely to be beyond any individual's control. Yet individual fat people or parents of fat children are at fault for lacking willpower and self-control. Similarly reports on the so-called 'obesity epidemic' are steeped in biomedical terminology but also something that could be eliminated by 'simply relying on common sense' (Boreo, 2013: 372). These contradictions are likely to be difficult for families to navigate and may feed into the feeling of confusion that can often be experienced with regard to what the latest advice is on diet, health and weight. This issue relates to another media genre that has become a common feature of our society, that of the health promotion campaign.

Anti-fat campaigns

As Lupton suggests, fatness is the latest 'supposedly preventable condition targeted in social marketing campaigns' (2014: 32). In January 2009, the Department of Health introduced the Change4Life campaign aimed at parents which formed part of the government's childhood obesity prevention strategy. A year later it presented its Start4Life campaign aimed at parents of very young children. There is much research on the usefulness or otherwise of such public health promotion campaigns, however Lupton (2014) raises some important issues with regard to campaigns which specifically target fatness. Firstly, she argues that low uptake on the advice on offer in these campaigns can often be because families are weary of the constant changes in 'expert advice'. Furthermore, some families object to being reproached by people who understand very little about the realities of their lives.

Secondly, she draws attention to the way these types of campaigns oversimplify behaviour change. Change4Life for example offers the following advice to parents: 'Get them back to a healthy weight with a few simple changes to help them eat more healthily and be more active' (DoH, 2009). As Lupton argues, what is lacking 'is an awareness of the complexity of individuals' health-related behaviours and their embeddedness in historical, economic, cultural, and social contexts' (2014: 39). Finally, she highlights how such campaigns never acknowledge that some of the information they contain is subject to dispute. As Lupton contends:

> Medical and epidemiological pronouncements on the health risks of fatness are often inaccurate, distorted and exaggerated, transforming speculative ideas on risk and 'obesity' into scientific fact. (2014: 40)

Fat science and the media

The media provide their audience with a range of so-called facts about obesity, which are presented as truths. What is generally not acknowledged, however, is that much of this fat science has been filtered or distorted to fit a purpose. Just as we have selected research to support our arguments here in this chapter so too have the government, media, diet and fitness industries carefully selected theirs.

One significant issue with the way fat science is presented in the media is that a lot of the research used is from epidemiological studies, where data tend to be obtained from existing large health surveys. For example, while a link might well be made between a high BMI and mortality this does not necessarily mean that it was body fat which killed people (Oliver, 2006). As Guthman contends, 'several of the tools used to describe and represent the "obesity epidemic" confuse the relationship between size and illness' (2013: 264) to present obesity as a health problem. She further suggests that some of the tools used to obtain so-called facts about fatness in the population can 'paint the picture in ways that may over-dramatize some elements and under-specify others' (ibid.), which she argues can exclude other valuable conceptualisations of fatness and narrow the scope of any solutions put forward.

Another issue in the way that the media select their research is that journalists will always 'favour studies that lend themselves to sensational headlines' (Boero, 2013: 374).

CASE STUDY 10.1   EXPLORING THE MEDIA

The following headline from the *Sun* newspaper (McDermott, 2016) provides just one of many examples:

> HONESTY IS BEST POLICY – GPs must TELL patients they're fat and prescribe weight-loss classes – to 'SAVE the NHS billions' ...
>
> ... Writing in the *Lancet*, researchers said GPs should stop worrying about offending tubby Brits ...

Fat blame

Fatness is predominately seen as blameworthy and deserving of censure. Lawrence (2004) suggests that there are two forms of blame relating to fatness: individual and systemic blame. However, as this chapter considers the fat child we discuss a third form, that of parental blame. As Sims-Schouten and Cowie indicate, it remains the fact that academic research and government focus still make associations 'between [bad] parenting styles and diet and weight in children' (2016: 452).

Individual blame

Individual blame is considered to be a personal problem that can be rectified through changing personal habits, such as through diet and exercise. As mentioned previously, terms such as 'obese' and images of fatness, such as a fat child eating chips, portray it as self-inflicted. Kirkland (2008) argues that it is common for fatness to be seen simply as personal choice and the attitude of society is that if the person wishes to avoid discrimination then they should lose weight. For example, when a fat person cannot fit into a seat at the cinema it is considered to be because of their size, not because of a lack of variety in seating to accommodate different body sizes. Huff (2009) highlights another example whereby airlines charge some customers for two seats, demonstrating again that the blame is placed on the individual as opposed to the airlines for failing to recognise the diversity in body size of the population it serves. As Pritchard (2014) importantly points out, we cannot expect to be a society where everyone is of a similar size or shape. While thinness may well be perceived as being of universalistic value, it rests on questionable assumptions about health benefits and is full of implicit ideals around body norms (Rich and Evans, 2005). As such, we argue that it is unrealistic for people to be expected to live in a built environment that only caters for this ideal.

Parental blame

With reference to the fat child the blame shifts to the parents, in particular the mother (Kokkoknen, 2009; Boero, 2013). The mother is still often viewed as a homemaker and responsible for what her children eat and how they are raised. For example, Eberstadt (2003) suggested that working mothers were more likely to have fat children and indicated that one reason for this was that children were being left to their own devices at home after school, while their mothers were at work, and thus exposed to full cupboards and refrigerators. Parent blame has even gone to the extreme that some fat children have been taken into care as their fatness has been seen as a form of child abuse. In 2014 police in Norfolk, in the United Kingdom, arrested the parents of an 11 year-old boy who weighed 15 stone (Quinn, 2014). Interestingly, however, as Herndon (2014) argues, the potential psychological damage caused by the child's experience of being removed from their home was overlooked.

Parent blaming is not unique to fat children; they, especially mothers, have commonly been blamed for a wide variety of social problems (Boero and Thomas, 2016). It is common, for example, for parents to be blamed if their child has Attention Deficit Hyperactivity Disorder (Singh, 2004), and parents, in particular mothers, have also previously been blamed if their child had autism. The 'refrigerator mother' was a label coined in the 1950s for mothers of children with autism. Their parenting skills, in particular their supposed lack of an emotional bond with their child, were blamed for their child's impairment. Kokkonen (2009) points out that mothers of fat children have also been blamed for their children's size because they were unable to create an emotional bond with them.

CASE STUDY 10.2   EXPLORING THE MEDIA

Many of the attitudes that we develop towards the children and families we work with stem from our engagement with the media. It is therefore important for us to be able to recognise how we as practitioners have been influenced by the many distorted views that the media can present. The following is an extract from a national newspaper article:

IF YOU ARE THE PARENT OF A FAT CHILD, YOU ARE A BAD PARENT

Lazy, selfish parents would rather let their child shovel sweets into their gob than take them to the park

... So why do so many parents make their kids fat? Because they are, to put it bluntly, selfish and lazy.

Because they would rather give their kids quick rubbish than go to any effort to give them a healthy meal. Because they would rather have an easy life and say Yes to every whimsical demand from a five-year-old for chocolate for breakfast than say No and face the consequences.

Because they would rather leave their child to spend eight hours on an Xbox than go to the effort of taking them out to the park. Because they would prefer to shove sweets into their child's mouth than have to bother listening to them when they'd rather be watching TV or playing on their iPhone. (Hartley-Brewer, 2015)

As Kokkonen (2009) argues, parents are frequently negatively constructed in the media as lazy and selfish. Typically, this article fails to take into account other factors that can contribute to a child being fat and instead simply blames the parent. It is argued here that by doing this attention is diverted away from the social inequalities that exist in society (Boero, 2009).

Gordon-Larsen et al. (2006) point out that people living in poorer areas have less access to facilities that promote physical activity. The author of the newspaper article does not take into account why parents may not take their child to the park.

For example, O'Dea (2006) shows that families living in poorer areas often fear leaving their children to engage in physical activity in their local areas due to safety concerns. Parks found in more affluent areas, on the other hand, are better maintained and experience lower levels of anti-social behaviour (Gallo et al., 2014). The author of the newspaper article has no interest in exploring the complexity of the situation and instead prefers to make crude assumptions about how the parents of fat children raise their children.

Systemic blame

Lake and Townsend (2006) suggest that fatness is not simply about diet and physical activity; consideration needs to be made of the social systems involved. Systemic blame includes what Swinburn and Egger refer to as 'obesogenic environments' (2002: 292). An obesogenic environment is described as 'the sum of influences that the surroundings, opportunities, or conditions of life have on promoting "obesity" in individuals or populations' (ibid.). For example, poorly-maintained pavements and perceptions of safety in certain areas have been shown to affect physical activity (Lake and Townsend, 2006).

Lobstein and Dibb (2005) argue that the more adverts for junk food per hour on children's television, the higher the proportion of fat children. Lake and Townsend (2006) note that marketing strategies by food corporations, such as Cadbury, are a contributor to increased levels of childhood obesity, with children often being constructed as more passive and vulnerable to the influences of advertising (Boero, 2009). Lobstein and Dibb (2005) argue that precautionary measures need to be taken to reduce children's exposure to obesogenic marketing practices. Systemic blame helps to expose some of the social causes of fatness, shifting the blame from the individual.

The 'war on obesity'

The UK government has recently unveiled its 'Childhood Obesity: A Plan for Action' (HM Government, 2016). While it includes some important steps to, for example, tackle the amount of sugar being used in the food industry, it offers no suggestions to reduce poverty for families, despite the report itself drawing on studies that make the link between poverty and fatness. Furthermore, there are no recommendations to reduce fat stigma and fat prejudice despite, again, it using research that links fatness and mental health problems. Moreover, a number of its plans have the potential to increase body shame in children and young people, body shame being 'an acute affective experience stemming from perceptions of having failed to achieve the narrowly defined cultural standards of body size' (Webb et al., 2016:11). These recommendations include increased surveillance by health professionals, children being weighed at every opportunity, and professionals (such as early years practitioners) being trained in how to address children's weight problems with their parents. Such approaches promote the objectionable nature of fatness, which in turn fuels prejudice.

Where is the war on fat stigma?

Puhl and Suh argue that 'weight stigma is rarely considered in obesity prevention and treatment efforts' (2015: 182) despite there being evidence that suggests that fat stigma plays a significant role in bringing about behaviours that are said to cause fatness. The government's recent 'Childhood Obesity' policy discussed above, and other related programmes such as the National Child Measurement Programme (NHS, 2016), draw no attention to this; they are instead saturated by 'anti-fat sentiment' (Webb et al., 2016: 6) that will only encourage fat stigma for children and generate fat prejudice. Interestingly, Puhl and Latner (2007: 557) identified educators, parents and peers as the primary sources of fat prejudice in the lives of children, with Harrison, Rowlinson and Hill (2016) suggesting that fat prejudice can already be found in preschool-aged children. Any desire to improve the health of young children should therefore include efforts to address this.

Fatness and bullying

The fat child is often perceived to be an easy and common target for bullies (Weinstock and Krehbiel, 2009), which could potentially have long-term consequences for the victim. The World Health Organisation concurs, suggesting that fat children are at greater risk of being bullied and of social isolation (WHO, 2012). What is interesting, however, is that such an organisation is unable to recognise the role it plays in causing this. When a fat child is bullied it is their fat that is to blame, not society's treatment of and attitude towards fatness. The solution is therefore weight loss as opposed to tackling the stigma and prejudice associated with occupying a socially-unacceptable body. It should be recognised that the World Health Organisation contributes to the socio-political ideology that creates this problem, a problem where 'fat individuals are deemed wholly responsible for their "excess" and thus deserving of consequent stigmatisation' (Webb et al., 2016: 11).

Unfortunately, it would seem that there is a lack of attention given to identifying fat discrimination and oppression (Weinstock and Krehbiel, 2009). If we accept fatness as a difference and do not focus on blaming the individual, then we can begin to generate some 'efforts to combat anti-fat bias and its ill-effects' (Webb et al., 2016: 11).

Alternative discourse: The importance of other perspectives

During the past five decades an increasing number of people have been offering other perspectives on fatness to that of the obesity discourse. Cooper (1998) suggests that the emergence of fat activism and fat studies is about challenging cultural attitudes towards fatness, including the dominant model of obesity, which encourages the stigmatisation and discrimination of fat people (Cooper, 2016).

The size acceptance movement started in the USA in the late 1960s, with the emergence of the grassroots movement National Association to Advance Fat Acceptance (previously National Association to Aid Fat Americans NAAFA) (Wann, 2009). This social movement, along with the development of the academic discipline of fat studies, has gained momentum over the years, and in 2012 the first academic journal, *Fat Studies*, was launched by Routledge. Rothblum, the journal's editor, proposed that *Fat Studies* 'seeks no opposition to the simple fact of human weight diversity, but instead looks at what people and societies make of this reality' (2012: 3). Fat people, including fat children, have always existed and always will, but how we choose to make sense of fat bodies and respond to them is shaped by many things and it is important to examine these. Fatness is not simply a medical discourse.

To date, fat activism and fat scholarship have mostly focused on issues relating to fat women. With the ever-intensifying childhood obesity discourse it is important that fat childhoods are examined from other perspectives. As Boero and Thomas argue we need 'fat childhoods to occupy a more central place in fat studies' (2016: 93) because up until now there has been limited exploration.

Intersections

Fat studies is similar to, and intersects with, other academic disciplines such as gender studies, critical race studies, queer studies and disability studies. For example, Cooper (1998) describes how she has been influenced by disability studies and the disabled people's movement, and has found the social model of disability a useful tool in arguing for fat acceptance. She suggests that the social model of disability offers fat people a way of framing fat prejudice as it shifts the cause of the 'problem' from the person to society. Thus, as we have seen in Chapter 4, instead of seeing a person who uses a wheelchair as unable to access a building because their physical impairment means they cannot climb stairs, the person is disabled instead because the building has been designed as though everybody walks when they clearly don't; if the building had a ramp the person would not be disabled. Cooper (1997) draws upon the social model of disability in order to claim that the built environment does not reflect the diversity of body size. The difference here, however, is that, as discussed earlier, fatness is predominately perceived as blameworthy, whereas disability in general is not. This hinders any opportunities for fat acceptance as a person is expected to lose weight in order to have the same access to facilities and acceptance within society. Cooper (2016) suggests that using the social model of disability in fat activism helps to move beyond trying to normalise fat people and instead works to accommodate them in society.

QUESTIONS FOR REFLECTION

1. How does the newspaper article in the second case study make you feel about parents of fat children? Do you think the situation is this straightforward?

2. Reflecting on the newspaper article what other explanations can there be for families not engaging in physical activity or eating foods that are deemed to be healthier? How might this article impact on the way that practitioners relate to fat children and their families?

3. How might fat stigma affect children?

4. Are parents to blame for their fat children?

5. What are the social and political factors that impact on how we conceptualise and respond to fat children?

SUMMARY

The concept of the obese child is extraordinarily complex, much more so than the government, the media and the diet and fitness industries would have us believe. There are many forces at play including some that have been highlighted in this chapter. It is not as straightforward as merely asking all fat people to take up more physical activity and go on a diet, and we do not simply have fat children because they have 'bad parents'. What must be recognised, however, is that blaming individuals is much easier than tackling societal issues such as poverty and social inequality. Furthermore, we must acknowledge the harm that is done to the well-being of children and their families through individual blame.

In society fatness is perceived through the dominant discourse of obesity. Here fatness is presented as blameworthy and easily rectified through diet and exercise. In this chapter we have provided a critique of this discourse as it relates to the fat child and illuminated some forces at work in creating this discourse and the negative effects it can have on fat children and their families.

End of chapter glossary

- **BMI** (Body Mass Index) is often used as a measurement for indicating obesity.
- **Fat** is a term reclaimed by fat studies to identify bodily difference.
- **Obesity** refers to fatness within scientific literature and is often linked with the notion of greed, thus requiring prevention.

- **Prejudice** involves a preconceived opinion that is not based on fact.
- **Stigma** involves the assignment of disgrace to a particular personal characteristic.

Further reading

Boero, N. and Thomas, P. (2016) Fat kids, *Fat Studies*, 5 (2): 91–97.

Cameron, E. and Russell, C. (eds) (2016) *The Fat Pedagogy Reader: Challenging Weight-based Oppression Through Critical Education*. New York: Peter Lang.

Harrison, S., Rowlinson, M. and Hill, A.J. (2016) 'No fat friend of mine': young children's responses to overweight and disability, *Body Image*, 18: 65–73.

References

Boero, N. (2009) 'Fat Kids, Working Moms, and the "Epidemic of Obesity": Race, Class and Mother Blame'. In E. Rothblum and S. Solovay (eds), *The Fat Studies Reader*. London: New York University Press.

Boero, N. (2013) Obesity in the media: social science weighs in, *Critical Public Health*, 23 (3): 371–380.

Boero, N. and Thomas, P. (2016) Fat kids, *Fat Studies*, 5 (2): 91–97.

Burkhauser, R. and Cawley, J. (2008) Beyond BMI: the value of more accurate measures of fatness and obesity in social science research, *Journal of Health Economics*, 27 (2): 519–529.

Cooper, C. (1997) Can a fat woman call herself disabled?, *Disability and Society*, 12 (1): 31–42.

Cooper, C. (1998) *Fat and Proud: Politics of Size*. London: The Women's Press.

Cooper, C. (2016) *Fat Activism: A Radical Social Movement*. Bristol: Hammer On Press.

Department of Health (DoH) (2009) *Change4life*. Available at www.nhs.uk/change4life-beta/your-childs-weight/home (last accessed 29 March 2017).

Erberstadt, M. (2003) The fat child problem, *Policy Review*, 117.

Gallo, G.R., Townsend, G.T. and Lake, A.A. (2014) Exploring urban parks and their peripheral food environments using a case study approach: young people and obesogenic environments, *Urban Design International*, 20 (1): 1–16.

Gard, M. and Wright, J. (2005) *The Obesity Epidemic: Science, Morality and Ideology*. London: Routledge.

Gordon-Larsen, P., Nelson, M.C., Page, P. and Popkin, B.M. (2006) Inequality in the built environment underlies key health disparities in physical activity and obesity, *Paediatrics*, 117 (2): 417–424.

Guthman, J. (2013) Fatuous measures: the artifactual construction of the obesity epidemic, *Critical Public Health*, (23) 3: 263–273.

Harrison, S., Rowlinson, M. and Hill, A.J. (2016) 'No fat friend of mine': young children's responses to overweight and disability, *Body Image*, 18: 65–73.

Hartley-Brewer, J. (2015) If your child is fat then you are a bad parent, *Telegraph online*. Available at www.telegraph.co.uk/news/health/11985974/If-your-child-is-fat-then-you-are-a-bad-parent.html (last accessed 30 March 2017).

Herndon, A. (2014) *Fat Blame*. Lawrence: University Press of Kansas.

HM Government (2016) *Childhood Obesity: A Plan for Action*. London: HMSO.

Huff, J.L. (2009) 'Access to the Sky'. In E.D. Rothblum and S. Solovay (eds), *The Fat Studies Reader*. London: New York University Press.

Kirkland, A. (2008) Think of the hippopotamus: rights consciousness in the fat acceptance movement, *Law & Society Review*, 42 (2): 397–432.

Kokkoknen, R. (2009) The fat child – a sign of 'bad' motherhood? An analysis of explanations for children's fatness on a Finnish website, *Journal of Community and Applied Social Psychology*, 19 (5): 336–347.

Lake, A. and Townsend, T. (2006) Obesogenic environments: exploring the built and food environments, *Journal of the Royal Society for the Promotion of Health*, 126 (6): 262–267.

Latner, J.D. and Stunkard, A.J. (2003) Getting worse: the stigmatization of obese children, *Obesity: A Research Journal*, 11 (3): 452–456.

Lawrence, R.G. (2004) Framing obesity: the evolution of news discourse on a public health issue, *Harvard International Journal of Press/Politics*, 9: 56–75.

Lobstein, T. and Dibb, S. (2005) Evidence of a possible link between obesogenic food advertising and child overweight, *Obesity Reviews*, 6: 203–206.

Lupton, D. (2014) 'How do you measure up?': assumptions about 'obesity' and health-related behaviors and beliefs in two Australian 'obesity' prevention campaigns, *Fat Studies*, 3 (1): 32–44.

McDermott, N. (2016) GPs must prescribe free weight watchers sessions to fat patients to save the NHS billions each year, *Sun online*. Available at www.thesun.co.uk/living/2040836/gps-must-prescribe-free-weight-watchers-sessions-to-fat-patients-to-save-the-nhs-billions-each-year/ (last accessed 30 March 2017).

Monaghan, F.L., Colls, R. and Evans, B. (2013) Obesity discourse and fat politics: research, critique and interventions, *Critical Public Health*, 23 (3): 249–262.

NHS (2016) *National Child Measurement Programme – England 2015-16*. Available at www.content.digital.nhs.uk/catalogue/PUB22269 (last accessed 30 March 2017).

O'Dea, A.J. (2006) Prevention of child obesity: 'First do no harm', *Health Education Research*, 20 (2): 259–265.

Oliver, J.E. (2006) Fat Politics: The Real Story Behind America's Obesity Epidemic. New York: Oxford University Press.

Oxford University Press (OED) (2004) *Oxford English Dictionary* (3rd edition). Oxford: Oxford University Press.

Pritchard, E. (2014) Body size and the city: creating an inclusive built environment using universal design, *Geography Compass*, 8 (1): 63–73.

Puhl, R. and Latner, J. (2007) Stigma, obesity, and the health of the nation's children, *Psychological Bulletin*, 133 (4): 557–580.

Puhl, R. and Suh, Y. (2015) Health consequences of weight stigma: implications for obesity prevention and treatment, *Current Obesity Reports*, 4: 182–190.

Quinn, B. (2014) Police defend decision to arrest obese boy on suspicion of neglect. *Guardian online*. Available at www.theguardian.com/uk-news/2014/jun/06/police-defend-arrest-parents-obese-boy-suspicion-neglect (last accessed 30 March 2017).

Rich, E. and Evans, B. (2005) 'Fat ethics': the obesity discourse and body politics, *Social Theory and Health*, 3 (4): 341–358.

Rothblum, E. (2012) Why a journal on fat studies?, *Fat Studies*, 1 (1): 3–5.

Rothman, K. (2008) BMI-related errors in the measurement of obesity, *International Journal of Obesity*, 32: 56–59.

Sims-Schouten, W. and Cowie, H. (2016) Ideologies and narratives in relation to fat children and bullies, 'easy targets' and victims, *Children and Society*, 30: 445–454.

Singh, L. (2004) Doing their jobs: mothering with Ritalin in a culture of mother-blame, *Social Science and Medicine*, 59 (6): 1193–1205.

Swinburn, B. and Egger, G. (2002) Preventive strategies against weight gain and obesity, *Obesity Reviews*, 3 (4): 289–301.

Wann, M. (2009) Foreword. In E. Rothblum and S. Solovay (eds), *The Fat Studies Reader*. London: New York University Press.

Webb, J., Fiery, M. and Jafari, N. (2016) 'You better not leave me shaming!': conditional indirect effect analyses of anti-fat attitudes, body shame, and fat talk as a function of self-compassion in college women, *Body Image*, 18: 5–13.

Weinstock, J. and Krehbiel, M. (2009) 'Fat Youth as Common Targets for Bullying'. In E.D. Rothblum and S. Solovay (eds), *The Fat Studies Reader*. London: New York University Press.

World Health Organisation (WHO) (2012) *Population-based Approaches to Childhood Obesity Prevention*. Geneva: WHO.

World Health Organisation (WHO) (2016) *Facts and Figures on Childhood Obesity*. Available at www.who.int/end-childhood-obesity/facts/en/ (last accessed 30 March 2017).

INDEX